CONTENTS

ACKNOWLEDGMENTS

Thanks are due Jim Magruder, Richard Sine, Bill Welch, and Wayne Youngblood for taking the time to answer questions, provide suggestions, and clarify details. Thanks to Austin Friese for helping with some of the illustrations.

Special thanks to Ken Beiner of Showcase Stamps in Wheat Ridge, Colorado, for his assistance with the illustrations and for his ongoing insights and suggestions as the project progressed.

I am especially grateful to editor/publisher Dorothy Harris for her guidance, encouragement, and support, without which this book would not have been possible.

Once again, thanks to my wife, Susan, who helped keep the project pointed in the right direction.

INTRODUCTION

We put a stamp on a letter, we mail it, and two or three days later it arrives. We do it all the time and never give it a second thought. It's all so simple. But it was not always that way.

There was a time when a person had to present each letter at the post office so that its postage could be calculated; a separate fee existed for each destination. And the cost could be as high as half a day's wages.

Sir Rowland Hill is credited with inventing the postage stamp in the late 1830s as part of his plan to reform the British postal system and establish uniform postage rates. At the time, the cost of sending a letter was calculated by a combination of weight and distance, resulting in a hodgepodge of fees, one from every individual point in Great Britain to every other point. The expense of sending a letter was so great that the average person rarely sent one.

Sir Rowland Hill.

People depended on writing to communicate in those days. There was no telephone, fax, or E-mail. And the high cost of postage inhibited communication, both business and personal. At that time, people had the option of prepaying letters—in which case the postmaster marked the letter paid by pen or handstamp—or sending them collect, which many did. Senders felt that since recipients were the ones who benefited from receiving a letter, they should pay for it. If the recipients refused the letter—which they often did—the post office was out the cost of transporting it.

Rowland Hill proposed a uniform fee—one penny—for any letter sent anywhere in the kingdom, this fee to be collected in advance. He reasoned that a uniform rate structure would reduce paperwork, increase efficiency, and encourage people to send more letters. Hill proposed that a small piece of paper evidencing prepayment of postage be attached to each letter at the time of mailing, and thus the postage stamp was born. Stamps would also tighten accountability, since postmasters would have to account for every stamp sold. Under the previous system of marking letters "paid" by pen stroke, there was little to prevent a postmaster from pocketing postage. Prepayment of postage would also eliminate the inefficient collect system. What really made Hill's proposal revolutionary was his recommendation to slash the cost of mailing a letter from an average cost of ninepence to one penny—an 89 percent reduction! Critics ridiculed Hill and warned that if implemented, his ridiculous scheme would lead to the ruination of the postal system. But Britain really had no other choice. The existing postal system was so burdensome on the public, so constraining on commerce, that it had begun to be a drag on the economy. So the British gave it a try, and to their amazement, it worked. The volume of mail increased steadily, and the

The Penny Black at left; contemporary British definitive at right.

postal system did not collapse as predicted. Queen Victoria knighted Hill for his contribution to creating the modern postal system. But philatelists around the world remember Sir Rowland Hill for inventing the postage stamp.

The world's first postage stamp (1840) featured a finely engraved profile of the young Queen Victoria together with the words "Postage" and "One Penny." Printed in black, it became known as the Penny Black. The name "Great Britain" did not appear on the Penny Black—only the simple, elegant portrait of Queen Victoria. To this day, Great Britain remains the only nation in the world that does not print its name on its postage stamps. Nor is it required to—a tribute to the contribution it made by introducing the modern postage stamp.

Before 1845, the United States shared Britain's original confusing system of hodgepodge postal rates based loosely on distance and weight. But in 1845, Congress followed Britain's lead and established uniform rates of postage for the United States. Letters traveling less than 300 miles cost 5 cents per half ounce; those traveling farther than 300 miles cost 10 cents per half ounce. In 1847, the United States issued its first postage stamps, although prior to that time several postmasters had issued provisionals (stamps issued locally by postmasters) as the success of the Penny Black became known.

Sir Rowland Hill's idea caught on quickly, and in no time nations all over the world began issuing postage stamps. And not long after, people began collecting them. They collected stamps because of their artwork and beauty and because stamps piqued their curiosity about faroff and mysterious-sounding places—Mauritius, St. Helena, Sierra Leone—places they'd never heard of, places they never suspected existed, places they suddenly hungered to know more about. Stamps provided tangible evidence of a broader world, something from faroff and exotic places—Mozambique, Manchukuo, Tristan Da Cunha—that one could hold in their hand. These elements of beauty and mystery fascinated early collectors, and continue to fascinate collectors to this day.

Stamp collectors know an amazing amount of trivia about world geography and history, all from postage stamps. They know these facts because stamps, especially commemoratives, reveal the essential kernels of a nation's history, geography, and notable personalities. They are a window into its culture. Every time one turns the pages of a stamp album, history unfolds. Kings, presidents, and dictators. Heros, despots, and idealogues. Scientists, explorers, and great thinkers. Authors, musicians, and artists. Events, places, flora and fauna. They're all waiting to be discovered and enjoyed on postage stamps.

PHILATELY

The term "philately" (stamp collecting) comes from the Greek *philos* (loving) and *ateleia* (exempt from tax), and refers to the fact that a postage stamp prepays a fee, rendering a letter free of tax (so to speak) to the recipient. Philately is more encompassing than just the collecting and mounting of stamps. It includes an interest in and the study of all things stamp-related—covers, postal history, design and production, and so forth. It's a widespread and well-established hobby, with collectors in every nation of the world and roots going back more than 150 years. A highly organized and stable international market gives stamps liquidity matched by few other hobbies.

The United States Postal Service estimates that 22 million Americans collect stamps. Most of these are casual collectors who don't necessarily save every stamp that's issued, belong to a philatelic society, or attend stamp shows. You may be one of these and not realize it. Of the 22 million, there are perhaps 250,000 serious collectors who own albums, belong to one or more national philatelic societies, or subscribe to one or more of the four philatelic weeklies (how many other hobbies boast *four* weekly newspapers?).

This book is organized to familiarize you with the hobby of philately and give some insight into how philatelists think. As you proceed through the chapters, you will acquire the essential vocabulary, learn about the essential tools, and learn how to use a stamp catalogue, how to protect your stamps, how to access additional philatelic resources, and how to go about selling your stamps if that's what you want to do. By the time you're through, you will have a grasp of the fundamentals and know how a philatelist thinks. The Bibliography contains titles of books that delve more deeply into specific subjects.

Stamps are small in relation to most other objects, and because stamps are small, philatelists tend to be detail-oriented. To think like a philatelist, you must pay attention to detail—type of printing, type of paper, type of watermark, type of perforations, centering, and hinging. All have a bearing on value.

Philatelists tend to be precise and analytical. Philately has evolved an extensive technical vocabulary to describe detail. The basic terms are defined in the essential vocabulary in the next chapter. Additional terms are used throughout the text. Consult the glossary at the end of the book as you encounter them.

Philatelists possess inquiring minds. Curiosity and acquisitiveness drive them. When a philatelist looks at a stamp, he or she wants to know what it is, where it comes from, when it was made, which details—if any—distinguish it from others of similar appearance, if it is rare, if it is in premium condition, if it has been altered, and what it is worth. He wants to know about its place in history and its place in his collection. He wants to know as much as he can about a stamp.

Most of us use stamps daily, or at least receive mail bearing stamps, but never give them much thought. By the time you have finished this book, you will understand how philatelists perceive these small bits of paper, and you, too, will see stamps differently. Perhaps you will be bitten by the collecting bug. Perhaps, the next time you hold a stamp in your hands, you, too, will regard it as a small treasure.

ESSENTIAL VOCABULARY

Below appear the terms which you will encounter most frequently and which you should become conversant with in order to carry on a conversation with a philatelist or stamp dealer.

TYPES OF STAMPS

A stamp is a bit of paper that evidences the pre-payment of a fee, most often postage. Basic types of stamps include:

Postage stamp—the most common type of stamp, used to evidence prepayment of postage. The term "postage stamp" is used to distinguish it from other types of stamps such as revenue stamps and trading stamps.

Definitive—issued for use on everyday mail. Usually issued in a series of various denominations and available over an extended period of time. Definitives are also known as regular issues.

Definitive stamps.

CHAPTER 2

Commemorative stamp.

Commemorative—a special stamp issued to honor a specific event, personality, or anniversary, and typically available for only a limited time, usually six to eighteen months.

Special occasion stamp—not really a definitive or commemorative. Examples include Christmas stamps and Love stamps.

Special occasions stamps.

Airmail—a stamp intended primarily for use on airmail.

Special delivery—a stamp intended for use on special delivery mail.

Official—a stamp valid for use only by a government agency and intended for use only on official mail.

Official stamp.

Postage due stamp.

Semipostal stamp.

Nondenominated stamp.

Computer-vended stamp.

Postage due—a stamp used to indicate that postage was underpaid by the sender and postage is due from the addressee.

Semipostal—a stamp for which only part of the purchase price applies toward postage; the balance is collected for some other purpose, often a charitable cause. Semipostals are usually denominated by two figures; the first is the amount valid for postage, the second is the amount allocated for the other purpose, e.g. 50c+20c. The United States does not issue semipostals.

Nondenominated—a stamp without a numerical denomination. The denomination is usually represented by a letter such as A, B, C, and so forth. Nondenominated stamps are most often transitional issues printed when a rate increase is anticipated but before the actual new rate is known.

Computer-vended postage—stamps dispensed by vending machines that imprint the denomination at the time the stamp is vended, usually on security paper containing a preprinted background.

Postal stationery—stationery sold by a postal service usually, but not always, with

Postage meter.

Revenue stamp.

imprinted postage. Postal stationery includes postal cards, stamped envelopes, and aerogrammes (air letters).

Meter—evidence that postage has been paid applied by postage meter machine such as those manufactured by the Pitney-Bowes Company.

Revenue—a stamp used to indicate the payment of a tax or fee; sometimes referred to as a fiscal. Examples include waterfowl hunting stamps, documentary stamps, playing card stamps, and cigarette stamps. Postage stamps are occasionally used for revenue purposes, most notably in countries of the British Commonwealth.

Cinderella—a general, all-encompassing term applied to any stamplike item not valid for postage,

Cinderellas.

Sheet stamp.

Coil stamp.

Booklet stamp.

such as exhibition labels, Christmas seals, and advertising fantasy issues.

Sheet stamp—a stamp issued in sheet form. Sheet stamps usually have perforations on all four sides, unless the stamp was issued imperforate or unless the stamp borders the edge of the pane and contains a straight edge.

Coil stamp—a stamp issued in roll form. Coil stamps have straight edges on opposite parallel sides.

Booklet stamp—a stamp issued in booklet form. Booklet stamps usually, but not always, have one or more straight-edged sides.

Self-adhesive—a stamp that can be peeled from its backing and attached to a cover (envelope) without being moistened.

Souvenir sheet—a sheet, usually small, containing one or more stamps, usually bearing a commemorative marginal inscription, and usually

Souvenir sheet.

15

issued for some special event or occasion. Stamps in souvenir sheets are valid for postage.

Miniature sheet—a smaller-than-normal sheet (pane) of stamps, often containing ten or twenty stamps, and not necessarily issued for some special event.

PRINTING METHODS

Intaglio—also known as engraving. A method of printing in which the design is engraved (recessed) into a metal plate. Ink fills the recesses and, when the stamp is printed, forms small ridges on the paper. Engraving can be identified by magnifying glass or by running a finger over the surface of the stamp and feeling the ridges.

Lithography—in some cases known as offset printing. A printing process using photographically etched plates. In some cases the image from the metal plate is offset onto a rubber-like blanket before being impressed on paper, hence the term "offset printing." Images are broken up into a series of dots in order to achieve tonal gradation. Color lithography involves mingling areas of dots from several plates, each printing a separate color, in order to achieve the effect of full color. The dot structure is visible under a magnifying glass.

Photogravure—also known as gravure printing. As in lithography, a gravure plate is also made by the photosensitive process; in photogravure, however, the ink lies in small recesses and is very thinly applied. Tones are achieved by varying the depth of the recesses and thickness of the ink. The image is broken up into a series of fine points that keep the paper from being pressed into the recesses. The dot structure in photogravure is usually much finer than that of lithography. The difference is apparent under a 10-power magnifying glass.

Typographed—also known as letterpress. The oldest form of printing. A method of printing in which the ink sits atop raised type and is transferred directly to paper.

BASIC TERMS

Mint—a stamp that has not been used (canceled). Often used in a stricter sense to mean a never-hinged, post-office-fresh stamp; however, there is no hard-and-fast rule. In this book, "mint" refers to an uncanceled stamp with gum.

Unused—a stamp that has not been used (canceled). Frequently used—mostly in auction catalogs and advertising—to indicate that an uncanceled stamp has no gum. When using a stamp catalogue or buying stamps, make sure you understand the specific meaning of the term as it is used in each context.

Uncirculated—a coin-collecting term never applied to stamps.

Used—a stamp that has been canceled.

Postally used—a stamp that has been used on mail as originally intended, as opposed to having been canceled to order (CTO) or used for revenue purposes. Advanced collectors generally disdain CTOs, preferring postally used stamps, which they feel are more legitimate, having performed the duty for which they were intended. They also eschew postage stamps used for revenue purposes. Postally

Typical CTO cancel.

used stamps are almost always worth more than CTOs or revenue-canceled stamps.

Canceled to Order (CTO)—a term used to describe the mass cancellation (typically applied to full sheets by printing press) of remainders of mint stamps, which are then usually sold at a discount from face value. The United States Postal Service (USPS) does not sell CTOs; some—but not all—foreign governments do. Dealers buy discounted CTOs for use in inexpensive mixtures, packets, or approvals. CTOs are generally easy to spot. A neatly applied, nonobliterative, printed cancel on a foreign stamp with full original gum is a dead giveaway.

Precancel—a stamp canceled before being sold and intended for use by bulk mailers. Precancels save the post office the trouble and cost of having to postmark a multitude of individual pieces in a bulk mailing. Traditionally, precancels contained the name of the mailer's city and state between two parallel bars. In the 1970s the style evolved into just two black bars. Later, even the bars were omitted, and most precancels today contain no apparent

City and state precancel (top left), bars-only precancel (top right), service-inscribed precancel (left).

cancellation at all. Instead, they are "service-inscribed" according to their intended use, e.g. "bulk rate." Service-inscribed stamps are commonly used on "junk mail" because marketing surveys have shown that recipients open a higher percentage of mail when it bears a stamp (as opposed to a printed postage-paid imprint). Collectors of traditional (city and state inscribed) precancels generally don't expect gum on their stamps. However, collectors of mint service-inscribed precancels prefer that they have full original gum.

Pane—a stamp-collecting term for a finished "sheet" of stamps as purchased across a post office counter, as distinct from a press or production sheet, which usually contains multiple panes of stamps.

Selvage—the marginal area surrounding a sheet or pane of stamps. Sometimes spelled "selvedge."

Perforations—The rows of holes between stamps that facilitate their separation. Holes not completely punched through a stamp's paper are known as blind perforations or blind perfs.

Imperforate—A stamp lacking perforations. Before perforating equipment was invented, stamps were issued imperforate and separated by cutting. Modern self-adhesive stamps are usually imperforate. Edges lacking perforations on stamps such as coil stamps and booklet stamps are known as straight edges rather than imperforates. Perforated stamps unintentionally issued without perforations are known as errors.

Imperforate stamp.

Roulette—A philatelic term referring to a series of small slits applied between stamps to facilitate separation.

Rouletted stamp.

Cover—a philatelic term for envelope, usually with a stamp attached. The term "cover" implies that the envelope has gone through the mail. A stamp attached to a cover is referred to as being on cover.

First day cover (FDC)—a cover bearing a stamp that has been postmarked on the first day it was available for sale to the public.

Cachet—pronounced ka-SHAY; a decorative illustration usually appearing on the left side of a cover, usually in connection with a first day of issue or special event. Cachets may be printed, rubber-stamped, hand-painted, or applied by other means.

Block—four or more stamps arranged in a rectangle.

Plate block—a block of stamps on whose selvage appears the printing plate number(s).

Plate number coil (PNC)—a coil stamp on which a small printing plate number appears at the bottom. Plate numbers appear at the bottom of stamps

First day cover.

Plate block.

Plate number coil strip.

at predetermined intervals, e.g., every 24th, or 52nd stamp. PNCs are usually collected in strips of three or five with the numbered stamp occupying the center position in the strip.

Line pair—a pair of coil stamps on which a line appears between the stamps. On engraved, rotary-press coil stamps, lines are created by ink that fills the space where the curved plates join and is then printed in the same fashion as ink from recesses in an intaglio stamp design.

Line pair.

Se-tenant pair.

Se-tenant—two or more different stamp designs printed next to one another on a pane of stamps, a souvenir sheet, a booklet, or a coil.

Tête-bêche—two adjacent stamps, one of which is inverted in relation to the other.

Tagged—a stamp possessing a luminescent coating applied during printing. Usually invisible to the naked eye, tagging can be observed under ultraviolet light. Tagging may cover all or part of a stamp.

Overprint—printing applied to stamps after regular production for any number of reasons: to denote a special purpose (such as airmail), to commemorate something, as a control measure, etc. An overprint intended to change a stamp's face value is known as a surcharge. Overprints are not cancellations.

CONDITION

Realtors are fond of saying that the three main elements of property value are location, location, and location. In philately, rarity notwithstanding, the three main elements of value are condition, condition, and condition. The same stamp that sells for $500 in superb, never hinged condition can often be bought for $50 in faulty condition. It is fair to say that 90 percent of the value of the superb stamp represents a premium for condition.

Condition is the sum of a stamp's elements: gum, hinging, centering, margins, color, freshness, cancellations, perforations, and faults. Remember these key words.

CAUTION: Don't tamper with your stamps. Old stamps are fragile. Trying to improve their appearance is risky. You're likely to do more harm than good, even if you think you're being careful. Don't remove stamps from envelopes or postcards; the intact item may be worth more, by virtue of its postmark or other markings, than the stamps by themselves. And for the same reason, don't cut the corners off old envelopes. Don't attempt to separate stamps that are stuck together or stuck down to album pages; you'll only damage them and reduce their value. Don't attempt to clean stamps; again, you'll only reduce their value. Leave everything intact. Rely on an experienced person such as a stamp dealer to give you the best advice on how to proceed.

Gum

Gum is the single most important element of condition of a mint stamp.

Original gum (OG)—gum applied at the time of manufacture. Until late in the twentieth century, usually composed of gum arabic or dextrin, which are smooth and glossy in appearance. Some recent gums (such as polyvinyl alcohol gums) have a dull, matte-like appearance. Original gum is prized. Stamps with full original gum are worth considerably more than stamps with partial gum or no gum.

Tropical gum—gum that has been affected by high humidity, often losing its gloss, and often discolored, either uniformly or in spots caused by microorganisms.

Disturbed gum (DG)—often arising from an attempt to remove a stamp hinge by the application of moisture, a process that leaves the gum in a mess and can even warp the stamp.

No gum (NG)—lacking gum, the inference being that the stamp originally possessed gum, which was later removed; hence an inferior state of condition. Stamps issued without gum are referred to as without gum rather than no gum to make the distinction that they are "as issued" and not impaired.

Regummed (RG)—regumming is a process intended to improve the appearance and salability of a stamp by applying new gum to simulate original gum. Regumming need not be contemporary; it may have been done years before. In philately, unlike other fields where restoration is encouraged, any attempt to improve the appearance of a stamp by adding new gum or new perforations or to alter it in any way from its original state is frowned upon. Regummed stamps are regarded as damaged goods and held in such low esteem that they trade at enormous discounts, typically only 10 to 20 percent of catalogue value. The premium for original gum on stamps has led to the practice of regumming.

Hinging

Until the middle of the twentieth century, collectors used hinges to mount stamps, which is why so few early stamps survive without hinge marks. Today, collectors of mint stamps generally favor plastic stamp mounts because mounts do not affect gum. The better the state of a stamp's original gum, the more valuable the stamp.

Early stamp hinges were often just bits of ordinary paper attached with whatever glue was handy, usually utilitarian glues made to hold things together. As a consequence, old-time hinges are difficult to remove. At best, they disturb a stamp's gum when removed. At worst, they take a layer of the stamp's paper with them, leaving a thin spot (known as a thin). Early commercially produced hinges were little better. More often than not, they leave gum horrendously disturbed when removed. Frequently, the only way to remove an early hinge is to soak it off. Hinges have often been

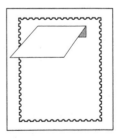

Stamp hinge.

soaked off to improve the look of a stamp. The back of a stamp without discolored, disturbed gum is more visually appealing than one with it or with an ugly hinge remnant. That's why so few early stamps are found with original gum.

Glassine hinges coated with light adhesives appeared later. They are known as peelable hinges. Peelable hinges generally cause no damage when carefully removed; nevertheless, they still leave hinge marks. Today, collectors want the best, most pristine examples of mint stamps possible, and that means never hinged stamps. Although lightly hinged (LH) stamps are not considered faulty, they are less desirable than never hinged stamps. Never hinged stamps command a premium; hinged stamps sell at a discount; no-gum and regummed stamps sell at substantial discounts.

CAUTION: Don't attempt to remove hinges from stamps unless you have experience. You're likely to cause damage and diminish the value of your stamps. Always use stamp tongs to handle stamps. Even the faint, colorless imprint left on gum by a finger on a humid day will reduce a stamp's value.

The descriptions of gum are followed by standard abbreviations where applicable.

Never hinged (NH)—a stamp that has never had a stamp hinge applied. Original gum is implied. A regummed stamp is never referred to as never hinged.

Lightly hinged (LH)—a stamp whose hinge mark is barely noticeable.

Heavily hinged (HH)—a stamp whose hinge (or part of it) is still in place, being so firmly attached that it is impossible to remove without damaging the stamp, or a stamp whose hinge has been removed, leaving a distinct and unappealing mark on the gum.

Part original gum (part OG)—possessing only part original gum, the missing portion presumably lost during the removal of a hinge or when applying

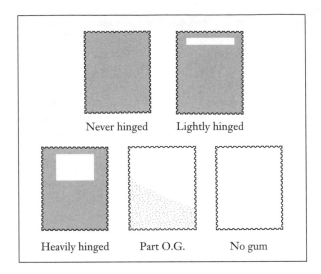

Never hinged | Lightly hinged

Heavily hinged | Part O.G. | No gum

moisture to loosen a stamp that had been attached to an album page by its own gum.

Disturbed gum (DG)—refer to the description in the previous section on gum.

Centering

What the condition of gum is to the back of a stamp, centering is to the front. Centering refers to the way in which a stamp's design is situated in relation to its margins. The more balanced the margins, the more visually appealing the stamp. Stamps with balanced margins are referred to as well centered. Stamps whose margins are not reasonably balanced are referred to as off-center or poorly centered. Collectors prefer perforations clear of a stamp's design and the design as evenly balanced within the margins as possible.

Nineteenth-century stamps—both U.S. and foreign—are notoriously poorly centered. In many cases, designers left almost no room between stamps, which resulted in perforations touching or cutting into designs on at least one side. Still, some issues are easier to find well centered than others. Modern stamps tend to be well centered, so finding nicely centered copies is usually not difficult. The

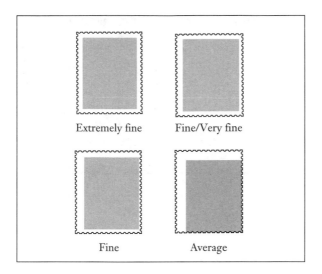

Extremely fine   Fine/Very fine

Fine   Average

characteristics of each issue must be taken into account when determining the grade of centering.

Standard grades of centering include:

Extremely fine (EF or XF)—well centered, margins almost perfectly balanced.
Fine/Very fine (F/VF)—moderately centered.
Fine (F)—poorly centered, perforations clear of the design.
Average (Avg.)—very poorly centered, perforations touching or cutting into the design; a real dog.

A variety of split grades, such as F–VF (fine to very fine), describe finer shadings. Catalogues typically list prices for only one grade, usually in the middle of the spectrum, often F–VF. Therefore, the actual price of a given stamp may be higher or lower than catalogue value, depending on its exact grade.

Other Elements

Margins—the size of a stamp's margins, as distinct from centering. Individual stamps possessing margins larger than normal for their issue are highly

The stamp at left has normal margins for issue; the stamp at right has jumbo margins.

prized by collectors. The larger than normal (for issue) the margins, the more desirable the stamp. Oversized margins are referred to as jumbo or boardwalk margins. Each stamp must be assessed in the context of the normal size of its margins.

Color—how vivid or pronounced color is within the range of shades known to exist for a given stamp. The older the stamp, the more important the intensity of color becomes. Old stamps tend to become drab with age. Papers tend to yellow; ink pigments tend to fade. Color is judged on how near it is to the issued state. A stamp's color must be measured against others of its kind, not against other issues that may be routinely boldly colored. Adjectives such as "vivid," "bold," "bright," and "intense" are used to describe stamps with premium color.

Freshness—how near to the original post office state a stamp is. Ideally, a stamp possesses "mint bloom" and pristine paper. Again, the older the stamp, the more difficult it is to find in a state of pristine freshness. Knowledgeable collectors avoid "toned" stamps, i.e., stamps turned yellowish or brownish, often from storage in albums or stock books made of cheap paper.

*Light cancels (left) are preferred; heavy cancels (right)
are avoided.*

Cancel (cancellation)—the ideal cancel being neat
and clear and neither distracting from nor obliterating the underlying design of the stamp. It is legitimate and contemporaneous to the stamp.
Collectors avoid favor cancels and contrived cancels, especially on expensive stamps. Stamps whose
mint and used prices are the same or nearly the
same are often encountered with bogus cancels
because clean used copies are more salable than no-
gum or heavily hinged mint copies. Hence the
emphasis placed on the words "legitimate" and
"contemporaneous." Colored and specialty cancels
can be worth a considerable premium on early
United States stamps. Check a specialized catalogue for more specific information. Pen cancels on
early issues sell at a discount. Pen cancels on modern stamps are considered faults, and the stamps
unsalable at any price. Revenue cancels are generally worth considerably less than postal cancels.

Perforations—ideally, having perforation teeth
(perfs) as balanced as possible within the limits of
the issue. Most early stamps have irregular perforations, which is not considered a fault. Sometimes
one or more perf teeth are shorter than the others
or missing entirely. They are referred to as short
perfs or pulled perfs. Issues with large or widely
spaced perforation holes often separate irregularly,
and for them irregular perfs are considered the
norm. Copies of such stamps possessing perfect

rows of teeth sell for a premium. The condition of perfs must be viewed within the context of what is usual for an issue.

Don't be too nit-picky about perforations. Most modern issues come with balanced perforations, and collectors really don't pay much attention to their condition unless it is visually distracting. Nor do they pay much attention to the condition of perfs on inexpensive stamps. The issue of perfect perfs applies mostly to early stamps and expensive stamps.

Reperforating is a process of adding perforations to improve the appearance of a straight-edged stamp, or to improve centering by trimming a margin and adding perforations. Reperforated stamps are worth only a small fraction of catalogue value.

Faults—tears, thins, pinholes, creases, surface scuffs, abrasions, stains, foxing, discoloration, glazed or tropicalized gum—anything that might be construed as damage—are considered major faults. Minor or trivial faults include such things as bent perforations or thinned perforations. The vast majority of nineteenth-century stamps are faulty. The earlier the stamp, the greater the likelihood it will be faulty. Stamps without faults are known as sound. The grades of condition that might otherwise apply to a sound stamp do not apply to a faulty stamp; faulty stamps go directly to the lowest price bracket.

Thins are usually the result of careless hinge removal and are visible from the back. Again, do not attempt to remove the hinge from a valuable stamp without the help of an experienced person. Creases may be visible to the naked eye, or visible only in watermark fluid; either way, they're considered faults. Sometimes stamps with faults are "improved." Creases are ironed out, discolorations bleached, pinholes and thins filled, scuffs and abrasions carefully colored to match original ink. Stamps that have been repaired or improved are considered faulty nonetheless. Faulty stamps and improved stamps are worth only a small fraction of catalogue value, typically 5 to 15 percent. The precise amount depends on the degree of the fault. The only exception is in the case of extremely rare stamps that do not exist in sound condition. Stamps with pieces missing are virtually worthless.

In many cases, faults and improvements are not obvious. It is prudent to check stamps carefully for any sign of tampering, especially when a significant amount of money is involved. (You'll find more about improvements in "Fakes and Forgeries.")

Natural inclusions (material embedded in paper during its manufacture), irregular perforations that are normal for an issue, and natural gum skips and gum bends (unless severe enough to have broken the paper fibers of the underlying stamp), while not technically faults, are elements avoided by the most demanding buyers. The absence of these elements generally increases the value of a stamp. Again, collectors of inexpensive stamps generally don't pay much attention to such things as natural inclusions and gum skips.

Elements such as straight edges (collectors prefer stamps with perforations on all four sides, except in the case of coil stamps, imperforates, and booklet stamps), heavy cancels, and exceedingly poor centering, while technically not faults, nevertheless reduce the value of a stamp to a small fraction of catalogue value.

In summary, condition is everything. Stamps are priced according to their merits; the higher the grade, the more valuable the stamp. Condition is more critical on early stamps and on expensive stamps. Inexpensive modern stamps are rarely scrutinized closely.

$\mathscr{E}$SSENTIAL TOOLS

STAMP TONGS. A pair of stamp tongs (collectors never call them tweezers) is the most basic philatelic tool. Stamp tongs provide more dexterity than human fingers, and they eliminate the possibility of damage from rough handling, moisture, oil, and the like. They come in a variety of styles and range in price from a couple of dollars on up. All dealers stock them. Don't use manicure tweezers or any other tool not specifically intended for handling stamps: some have sharp edges or ridges for gripping, which can cause damage when used to pick up stamps. As condition is the key element of stamp value, it is essential to guard against careless handling that might cause damage, however slight.

Stamp tongs.

PERFORATION GAUGE. It is nearly impossible to measure perforations accurately without a gauge.

When any of several elements (perforations,

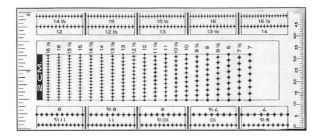

Perforation gauge.

watermark, color, paper, type of printing press) differ from one stamp to the next, each stamp is considered a distinct, collectible variety. A perforation
gauge is used to measure a stamp's perforations and
thus distinguish one perforation variety from
another. Most stamps exist perforated in only one
way, so measurement isn't necessary. A perforation
gauge makes it easy to identify those that come perforated in more than one way. Consult a stamp catalogue to learn what varieties exist for each stamp.

Perforations are measured by the number of
holes that appear within a space of 2 centimeters.
Perforated 10 means that 10 perforation holes
appear in 2 centimeters; perforated $10\frac{1}{2}$ means
$10\frac{1}{2}$ holes per 2 centimeters; and so on. When perforations are of the same size on all sides of a stamp,
the measurement is expressed as "perforated 11," or
whatever number is appropriate. Perforations are
the same on parallel sides of a stamp (except in a
few rare cases), but sometimes differ vertically and
horizontally, in which case they are known as compound perforations, and the measurement is
expressed in the form "perforated $10\frac{1}{2}\times11$," with
the first numeral referring to the horizontal gauge
and the second, to the vertical. Collectors generally
shorten the word "perforated" and say "perf 11,
perf $10\frac{1}{2}\times11$," etc.

Ninety-nine percent of perforation measurements are expressed to the nearest half or quarter
hole, e.g., $10\frac{1}{2}$ or $10\frac{1}{4}$. Some catalogue publishers
have begun expressing perforation measurements

This example is perforated 11×12. Note the different spacing of perforations horizontally and vertically.

for newly issued stamps decimally, e.g., perforated 11.2. Wisely, they're not revising previously published measurements into decimal expression, which would result in much confusion. However, since the trend for new issues seems to be decimal expression, it makes sense to get a gauge that measures in both fractions and decimals. *Linn's Stamp News* Multi-gauge is one of the best and costs only a few dollars.

The John Paul Jones commemorative, issued in 1979, exists perforated 11, perforated 11x12, and perforated 12. The first two types are worth less than half a dollar each; the perforated 12 variety is worth about $2,000 mint and $1,000 used.

WATERMARK DETECTOR. A stamp's watermark—or lack of watermark—is just as important as its perforations. A watermark is a mark impressed in paper during its manufacture. Watermarked paper is employed in stamp production as a security measure. Watermarks often appear on stationery and business paper and become visible when held up to

Watermark tray and fluid.

the light. Some stamp's watermarks are visible when held to light, but most are not, because of the small size of a stamp and the opacity of its printing ink. Watermarks on U.S. stamps are almost impossible to see without a watermark detector.

The traditional watermark detector is a black tray in which a stamp is placed facedown and covered with watermark fluid; the watermark then becomes visible. Tray and fluid cost only a few dollars.

CAUTION: Do not use water in a watermark detector. You'll lose the gum on mint stamps and diminish their value greatly. Use only watermark fluid designed specifically for use with stamps. Watermark fluid is inexpensive and available at any stamp dealer or by mail order from any stamp supply company.

TIP: A little fluid goes a long way. Put the stamp in the tray first, then add only as much fluid as necessary to moisten it and reveal the watermark. It is not necessary to drown the stamp in a tray full of fluid, then have to struggle to pour the excess back into the bottle without spilling it.

Watermark fluid doesn't dissolve stamp gum and dries almost instantly. Some individuals use lighter fluid in watermark trays. It works just fine; however, it leaves a slight, almost imperceptible oily residue, so it's best to avoid it. The inks of some British Commonwealth stamps are soluble in watermark fluid, so it's wise to consult a stamp catalogue before immersing such stamps. Watermark trays are also used to detect damage (thins, creases, etc.) and repairs, but more about that in "Fakes and Forgeries." Checking for watermarks may sound a bit complicated, but in practice it isn't. The United States used watermarked paper for postage stamps

Double Line (left), single Line (right)

between the years 1895 and 1915, so there's no need to check earlier or later stamps. Many foreign nations still use watermarked paper. Specialists prize inverted watermarks, omitted watermarks, and erroneously watermarked stamps—(such as the 1938 U.S. $1 Woodrow Wilson postage stamp inadvertently printed on paper watermarked USIR (United States Internal Revenue) intended for revenue stamps. The error stamp is currently worth about $300 mint and $70 used.

Optical-electric watermark detectors eliminate the need for fluid. Some collectors prefer them for that reason; however, optical-electric watermark detectors are costly ($100 and up) and work best on mint never hinged stamps and stamps without gum. Hinge remnants and disturbed gum tend to obscure watermarks and faults. Most collectors prefer the traditional method because it is inexpensive, portable, and invariably gives a reliable result.

MAGNIFYING GLASS. A good magnifying glass or jeweler's loupe is indispensable. It should be at least 10 power to adequately view secret marks, type markings, and other small detail.

ALBUM. Stamp collections are generally housed in albums, which range from entry-level basic to the highly specialized and expensive. Albums protect stamps, serve as means of organizing them, and provide a convenient way to view and enjoy them. Most albums feature printed illustrations on each page to indicate placement of stamps. Top-of-the-line hingeless albums come with plastic mounts preinstalled, so that all you do is insert stamps in their appropriate spaces. Specialty albums exist for nearly all countries, and for U.S. stamps and specialties such as plate blocks and plate number coils,. The best albums are loose-leaf to accommodate supplement pages, which album companies publish (usually annually) to enable collectors to keep their collections up to date. Some album pages are printed on acid-free or archival paper.

Don't be hasty or impulsive when choosing an album, especially an expensive one. Talk to other collectors and get the benefit of their experience before buying.

CAUTION: Never house stamps in variety-store photo albums, especially those with self-adhesive or wax-backed pages. The wax penetrates the stamps and in time ruins them, especially in hot climates. Even photo albums with "low-tack" adhesive can damage stamps over time. A good rule of thumb is: if something wasn't meant for stamps, don't use it.

TIP: Experienced collectors prefer album pages printed on one side rather than two because facing pages loaded with stamps tend to bind up on one another as pages are turned. If you must use double-sided pages, insert glassine interleaves between pages to avoid damage. They're available from stamp dealers and album publishers.

Advanced collectors, specialists, and exhibitors often prefer to make their own album pages, with as many or as few stamps per page as seems appropriate, and with as much or as little text as serves their purpose. Most album manufacturers offer quadrille-lined (faintly printed lines) blank pages, which make designing a layout easy. More and more computer software for making album pages is coming to market. Check advertising in philatelic periodicals for sources.

Albums for covers usually contain loose-leaf pages of clear plastic pockets into which covers are inserted for display. The best ones are made of mylar. Vinyl treated with softening agents (visible as an oily, iridescent film; the more softener, the more iridescence) should be avoided, as these agents have been known to leech the color out of some printing inks and to discolor stamps.

MOUNTS. Until the late twentieth century, stamp hinges were the mount of choice. Modern hinges consist of a small piece of glassine lightly gummed on one side. The hinge is folded, usually about one-third of the way from the top, the smaller flap lightly moistened (too much moisture will make the hinge difficult to remove later), and attached to the stamp near its top edge. Then the larger flap is moistened and attached to the album page. Hinges work well and are still the mount of choice for low-cost stamps and used

Stamp mount.

stamps. Few collectors use them for mint never hinged stamps because they leave a mark on gum when removed. Until the mid-twentieth century, no one paid much attention to hinge marks, but once the hobby began insisting on pristine gum, hinges for mint stamps fell out of favor.

Today, the mount of choice for mint stamps is the plastic mount. Plastic mounts are easy to use, protect stamps from hinging, frame them nicely against an album page, and lend a polished look to their presentation. Plastic mounts come in a variety of sizes to meet any conceivable need. Several different styles and brands exist. They're available from most dealers.

CAUTION: Always use a mount large enough to accommodate a stamp comfortably. Never try to force a stamp into a mount too small or too tightly fitting. Either you'll damage the stamp right then, or it will warp with the passing of time (plastic and paper expand and contract at different rates). Either way, you will have ruined the stamp. And be careful not to use too much saliva when moistening the back of a mount. Excess saliva will leak onto the gum, defeating the whole purpose of the mount. Never mount stamps or covers by taping or gluing them down, and do not use cellophane tape to secure the sides of plastic mounts.

ODDS AND ENDS. Glassine envelopes are used for storing stamps. They're inexpensive and come in a variety of sizes. Never use wax paper or clingy plastic kitchen wrap to house or store stamps. They usually do more harm than good.

Stock books are handy for organizing stamps awaiting mounting and for storing duplicates. Stock book pages consist of horizontal pockets created from manila, glassine, or clear plastic into which stamps can be slipped. Stock books are available in a variety of sizes.

Stock sheets are the loose-leaf version of stock book pages. They come punched for three-ring binders and several other types of binder. Display-style stock sheets are made of black or white card or plastic stock on which as few as one or as many as fourteen rows of clear plastic pockets have been attached. Some collectors use display-style stock sheets to house their collections instead of traditional album pages. They like the flexibility and convenience of stock sheets, and, indeed, there is much to recommend this system. Manila stock sheets are less expensive than plastic stock sheets and are more useful for storage than display.

Stock cards are small versions of stock sheets and are available in a variety of sizes, the most common of which measures $3\frac{1}{4} \times 5\frac{1}{2}$ inches and contains either one or two rows of pockets. They're useful for housing high-quality duplicates.

Plastic sleeves, sealed on three sides and open on the fourth, are used to house covers. They come in a variety of sizes. The best are made of mylar or polyethylene, both of which are much more inert than softened vinyl. Mylar sleeves are clear and rigid. Poly sleeves are slightly grayish in appearance, floppy rather than rigid, and much lighter if shipping or traveling is a consideration.

A color identification chart is useful, especially for those just getting started. Stanley Gibbons manufactures one of the best.

Ultraviolet light is used to detect luminescent coatings on stamps. Since the late 1960s, a variety of luminescent coatings have been utilized on stamps to trigger automated facing and canceling equipment. The stamps we use every day contain some type of luminescence, either in the paper or printed atop the design. This invisible coating, referred to by collectors as tagging, is visible under ultraviolet light and is important to the specialist. However, unless tagging varieties are important to you, an ultraviolet light may not be worth the expense.

TIP: if you buy an ultraviolet light, get a portable model that fluoresces *both* longwave and shortwave ultraviolet light. Savvy collectors favor the type used by gem and mineral collectors.

An identification guide is worth its weight in gold because before you can look up a stamp in a catalogue, you need to know its country of origin. Identifying stamps inscribed in Arabic, Chinese, Japanese, Korean, or Cyrillic characters is especially frustrating. Just because a stamp is inscribed in Cyrillic doesn't mean it comes from Russia. It might come from any of more than a dozen countries, including Armenia, Montenegro, and Bulgaria. You could spend all day flipping through a catalogue and still not figure out where it came from. Identification guides group illustrations of difficult-to-identify stamps by inscriptions, by heads (of state), by numerals, and by pictures. It takes only seconds to identify a stamp using one. Identification guides also contain a glossary of foreign expressions such as *autopaketti* (inscription on Finnish parcel post stamps) and *tasa* (inscription on postage due stamps of Uruguay) to make identification of specific kinds of stamps easy. Several brands are on the market. Most dealers carry at least one.

Philately has been blessed with a wealth of literature few other hobbies can match. During the past 150 years, thousands of knowledgeable collectors from all over the world have written books on just about every aspect of philately. No matter how esoteric or obscure your area of interest, you will almost certainly be able to find a philatelic reference specific to the subject—airmail stamps, postal cards, territorial post offices, Zeppelin mail, even books devoted to the study of a single stamp, such as Carroll Chase's exhaustive study of the three-cent 1851–1857 issue. You name it, there's likely a book on it. Out-of-print books are available from philatelic literature dealers, or you can borrow them from philatelic libraries. Consult the resource guide for their addresses.

Ken Wood's three-volume work *This Is Philately* is a wonderfully comprehensive encyclopedia of philately and an excellent and recommended general reference. It is scarcely possible to think of a term or subject not covered in its thorough 878 pages. Beginner and old hand alike find it useful.

The most basic reference work is the stamp catalogue. Every collector owns at least one. Catalogues are so important that the next chapter is devoted entirely to them.

Never hesitate to invest in books. A kernel of knowledge gleaned from one can mean the difference in buying or selling a stamp for pennies versus hundreds of dollars. Books are truly worth their weight in gold, not only in terms of knowledge but as collector's items themselves. Philatelic specialty books are usually printed in small press runs, typically 100 to 2,000 copies. They're often expensive new, but once out of print sell for multiples of their original cover price.

Subscribe to at least one philatelic weekly. It's the best way to keep current on the hobby. There are four in America: *Stamp Collector*, *Linn's Stamp News*, *Stamps*, and *Mekeel's Stamp News and Market Report*. They feature news, calendars of forthcoming issues, schedules of stamp shows across the nation, and loads of advertisements with current market prices. *Global Stamp News*, a hefty newspaper published monthly, is a must for anyone who collects foreign stamps. At the moment, there are two monthly magazines: *Scott Stamp Monthly*, and *U.S. Stamp News*. In addition, dozens of specialized societies publish monthly or quarterly journals. Foremost among them is the monthly *American Philatelist*, published by the American Philatelic Society. Check the resource guide for specifics.

$\mathscr{S}$TAMP CATALOGUES

A stamp catalogue is the basic reference to which all collectors turn time and again. The term "catalogue" in philatelic parlance takes on the connotation of a reference work rather than a publication from which you might order something, such as a Sears or L. L. Bean catalogue. It is usually—but not always—spelled "catalogue" rather than "catalog," perhaps to reinforce its role as a reference. Stamp catalogues provide two primary types of information: technical and pricing.

Scott Publishing Company publishes a highly respected annual series of catalogues that list, illustrate, and price virtually every general variety of postage stamp in the world. This *Scott Standard Postage Stamp Catalogue* is the most widely used stamp catalogue in America. Scott also publishes the *Specialized Catalogue of U.S. Stamps*, which lists, illustrates, and prices every U.S. postage stamp as well as Christmas Seals, revenue stamps, proofs, essays, and just about anything else stamp-related of significance or value. It is recognized as *the* authoritative reference for U.S. stamps and is indispensable for the U.S. collector. Scott catalogues are available at stamp dealers, in bookstores, and in most libraries.

Several other firms publish U.S. stamp catalogues or combination catalogue/price lists. The

Minkus catalogue utilizes its own numbering system. The *Brookman, Harris,* and *Mystic* catalogues use the Scott numbering system under license from Scott, and each has its own constituency. In addition to these, the Postal Service publishes a pocket guide, *The Postal Service Guide to U.S. Stamps,* which is noteworthy because it is illustrated in color. Check the bibliography for addresses.

If you develop an interest in collecting a foreign country's stamps, you'll want to consider a specialized catalogue for that country. As a rule, the most comprehensive foreign specialized catalogues are published in the countries of their stamps' origin. For example, *Gibbons* is the undisputed authority for Great Britain; *Michel* for Germany; *Yvert* or *Ceres* for France; Bolaffi for Italy; *Zumstein* for Switzerland, and *Edefil* for Spain. Foreign specialized catalogues cover the stamps of their nations in exquisite detail, listing, illustrating, and pricing stamps that are too esoteric for general catalogues. It is wise to have one of these, even if it's a few years old, just for the illustrations and technical information, which never change. The only drawback is that most foreign specialized catalogues are published in the language of their origin, not in English. Still, since most listings are illustrated and in philatelic shorthand, they are reasonably comprehensible. Check with your local dealer for these.

Specialty catalogues focus more narrowly still, providing more highly detailed information than general catalogues do. Examples include the *Durland Standard Plate Number Catalog* (for plate blocks) and the *Scott First Day Cover Catalogue and Checklist* (for FDCs). There are many others.

The first function of a catalogue is identification. Before using any catalogue, read the introduction carefully. You'll save yourself a lot of time and trouble. Although listings are user-friendly, they contain information of a technical nature often not understood by those unfamiliar with the intricacies and protocols of philately. Stamps are organized by country, and listed chronologically. Within a coun-

This stamp is known as Scott No. 292, Minkus No. CM24, and Michel No. 124.

try stamps are typically organized (although format varies from publisher to publisher) by type of stamp. Definitives and commemoratives are usually—but not always—grouped together, followed by semipostals, airmails, special deliveries, postage dues, officials, and so forth. Each stamp is assigned a unique number known as a catalogue number. Catalogue numbers are the shorthand of the hobby. Mention that you'd like to trade a used U.S. Scott No. 292 for a used Austria Scott No. 380 and the other party, whether in America or somewhere else in the world, will know precisely which two stamps you mean.

Each catalogue publisher has its own numbering system, so collectors mention both publisher and number, such as Scott No. 292, which is Minkus No. CM24, or Michel No. 124, all of which refer to the same stamp. The use of Scott catalogues is so widespread in the United States that catalogue numbers are understood to be Scott numbers unless otherwise indicated.

In addition to a catalogue number, each listing has an illustration, a design identifying number (or letters), description (denomination, color and/or subject), gauge of perforation, watermark (if any), method of printing (engraved, lithographed, etc.), date of issue, color of overprint or surcharge (if any), and a price for mint and used copies. Prices for plate blocks, PNCs, first day covers, and other collectible forms of an issue are listed directly below the main listing. Color shades, varieties, and errors are sublisted (usually indicated by a lower-case letter) below main listings.

T99 Abraham Lincoln

1909			Double Line Wmk.		Perf. 12
123	T99	2c	**carmine**	4.00	1.00
			on cover		3.00
			plate block (6)	100.00	—
			Imperforate		
124	T99	2c	**carmine**	25.00	15.00
			on cover		25.00
			plate block (6)	175.00	—
			Bluish Paper		Perf. 12
125	T99	2c	**carmine**	175.00	175.00
			on cover		325.00
			plate block	2,500.00	—

*Typical catalogue listing. Note the design
identifying number T99.*

Some catalogues list prices for both mint never
hinged and hinged condition. Prices are typically
for a middle-of-the-road grade such as F–VF (Scott
uses VF as its basic grade for pricing), with grades
higher or lower worth more or less, something the
user must factor on a case-by-case basis. Make sure
you know which grade the listed price refers to
when checking on a stamp's price. (More about
price later.)

Many stamps are identical in appearance but differ in watermark, perforation, or paper, hence the
need for design identifying numbers. The illustrated two-cent Lincoln design is identical on three
stamps, each of which has its own separate catalogue number (No. 123 through 125 in this hypothetical example). They all share the same design
identifying number (T99 in this hypothetical example). They range in value from a dollar to more
than a hundred dollars. In case this sounds confusing, only a few stamps are as complex as the two-

cent Lincoln. The vast majority consist of a single variety and have only one catalogue number.

The second function of a stamp catalogue is pricing. The intricacies of pricing are the most confusing, least understood element of stamp catalogues. Just remember, catalogues are general guides to pricing, not the final word on it, for a couple of reasons.

First, catalogues attempt to reflect actual market prices, they do not determine them. Supply and demand determine market prices. The financial section of your daily newspaper reports the prices of stocks; it does not determine them. Stamp catalogues perform the same function, except that they're published only once a year, rather than daily. During the course of the year, the stamp market moves according to its own rhythm, responding to a variety of factors, such as the state of the economy, supply and demand in foreign markets, and exchange rates. All kinds of things affect pricing between the publication of one edition of a catalogue and the next. For the most part, however, stamp prices are not volatile and catalogue prices remain reasonably reliable; nevertheless, always remember that the market is the final arbiter of price. Advertisements in philatelic publications are a good way to keep up-to-date on the market.

Second, unlike stocks, stamps vary physically from one another (condition), and, like gemstones, they are priced on an individual basis. Stamp retail prices are usually quoted in terms of discounts (or premiums) from catalogue that take into account each stamp's specific condition. For example, a severely impaired mint copy of the 1898 U.S. $1 Cattle in the Storm commemorative might retail for as little as $150, while a superb, never hinged copy can easily cost thousands of dollars. There are hundreds of combinations and permutations of condition, each priced according to its merits.

Market values for early nineteenth-century

stamps vary so often and so greatly from catalogue prices because most examples are faulty, while catalogue prices are for sound stamps. That catalogue prices are for sound stamps is clearly stated in every catalogue's introduction yet is routinely overlooked or ignored by catalogue users. The joy of discovering that the catalogue value of Aunt Esther's Bavarian States stamps is $1,000 is replaced by disbelief, anger, and frustration when you're told by a dealer that they're worth $50 because they're faulty. Bear in mind, the dealer is not trying to pull a fast one. There is little market for damaged stamps; serious collectors want sound examples. The only way to move damaged stamps is to discount to the bone. Catalogue prices are high for *sound* nineteenth-century stamps not because they are rare *but because they are rare in sound condition.* The more recent the issue, the greater the proportion of sound, high-quality examples.

Market price varies from catalogue price for another reason. Heretofore, we've talked about stamps of measurable individual value. There are thousands of others with no measurable individual value. Flag definitives on incoming daily mail are basically worthless. Nobody ever buys one individually from a dealer. People soak them off letters or obtain them from mixtures that sell by the pound. Still, regardless of how common it is, every stamp has a minimum catalogue value—typically fifteen cents—to cover a dealer's time and overhead for stocking and delivering it on demand. Think of it as a service charge. And in reality, fifteen cents probably doesn't even come close to covering the dealer's costs. Next time you're out shopping at a mall, make note of how many items you can buy for fifteen cents. Retailers just don't stock fifteen-cent items.

As mentioned before, retail advertisements for individual stamps, sets, and country collections in philatelic periodicals are helpful in getting a feel for the market. Prices realized that are published by stamp auction firms after each auction are also helpful in gauging the market. *Stamps Auction News* contains a digest of auction prices realized for key issues of the United States and selected issues of the world. Listings are arranged by catalogue number and contain grade and condition information together with prices realized, making it easy to compare at a glance what stamps in various grades have sold for.

In summary, stamp catalogues are the key reference tool in the hobby. Technical information remains constant; prices do not. Prices vary with era, country, and condition. Superb material often commands a premium, which can amount to as much as ten times catalogue or more. Impaired material sells for a discount, as little as a tenth of catalogue or less. The best way to get a feel for market prices is through contact with active collectors and dealers, by browsing buy and sell ads in philatelic periodicals, and by checking auction prices realized.

WHERE TO GET STAMPS AND OTHER RESOURCES

Collectors rely on a variety of sources for stamps and covers, including personal sources, post offices, local dealers, direct mail, auctions, stamp clubs and societies, and stamp shows.

PERSONAL SOURCES

A fresh supply of stamps arrives every day on incoming household and business mail. Much of it is collectible, and some of it has cash value. Dealers often pay $1 to $4 per stamp for sound, device-canceled (as opposed to pen-canceled) copies of priority mail and express mail stamps (no postage meters, please). They won't buy damaged copies, and they pay very little for pen-canceled copies. Leave stamps on cover until you have enough experience to know which ones can safely be removed.

PNC collectors love finding examples on cover, and junk mail offers a never-ending supply. There's also a cash market for PNC covers, especially those with rare numbers. Examine coil stamps on incoming mail for the tiny plate numbers that appear every so often at the bottom of stamps. You won't find many, but when you find one, leave the cover intact.

Look for high values ($1 denominations and up) on cover, interesting usages such as registered and certified mail, and errors. (More about errors in the chapter "Errors on Stamps.") Again, leave covers intact until you have enough experience to know which stamps can be removed without diminishing value.

Travel agencies often receive an abundance of foreign mail. Ask them to save covers intact for you. Ask friends, neighbors, and relatives to save covers for you and to check their attics, trunks, and basements for old letters or stamps. Businesses, state agencies, even historical societies often discard outdated correspondence (including covers) sometimes going back more than a century. These are fertile hunting grounds. Keep an eye open for anything unusual—Civil War covers (especially patriotic covers, POW covers, and anything with Confederate stamps), pony express covers, local posts, high denominations, out-of-the-ordinary markings (e.g., via aeroplane, censored), runs of correspondence from western settlers (especially with manuscript or fort postmarks), and anything of historical significance relating to an event or personality. Modern mail also offers opportunities. Keep your eyes open for covers from domestic Japanese internment camps, illustrated V-mail, POW mail (both U.S. or foreign), and covers from Vietnam, just to mention a few. As you learn more about philately and postal history, you'll better understand what to look for.

Often you can find stamps at flea markets and estate sales. A word of caution: flea market operators sometimes buy stamp dealers' unwanted remainders and resell them at their booths for more than they would otherwise cost you at a dealer. They prefer old, intriguing-looking albums to lure unwary buyers. Remember, being old doesn't auto-matically mean a stamp is valuable. Before taking a flyer, it's best to have a pretty good feel for the fundamentals of rarity and value. The caution notwithstanding, treasures are waiting to be found at flea markets and estate sales. Experienced buyers prefer large, untouched lots, especially nineteenth-century correspondences. Correspondences that appear innocuous to the uninformed—but are valuable by virtue of esoteric markings, origins or destinations—offer the best opportunity for profit. The key is knowledge, which enables you to recognize opportunity when it presents itself. The more knowledge you have, the better your odds of finding treasure.

It's not uncommon to discover an enclosure in a cover—and the tales they tell range from the mundane to the heart-stopping: flood, famine, Indian attacks, disease—and none of it filtered through the eyes of an historian. Few things can match the thrill of holding in one's hand an actual piece of history, for as you read the letter writer's words you cannot help but wonder, who were these people and what were their lives really like? And therein lies the fun.

POST OFFICES

The most obvious place to buy stamps is the post office. Most large cities (and many smaller ones) have philatelic centers that cater to stamp collectors. Philatelic centers usually stock a wide assortment of issues, many of which are not always available at regular windows. Clerks at philatelic centers usually have information on local clubs and upcoming shows and know who the local dealers are. You can also order stamps directly from the USPS Philatelic Fulfillment Service Center in Kansas City. Check the resource guide for the address.

Virtually every nation in the world maintains a philatelic agency from which collectors can order new and recent issues at face value. In addition, some foreign postal administrations have agencies in the United States from which collectors can obtain stamps at face value without having to send abroad. Most offer a standing-order service that allows you to receive new issues automatically against a deposit.

LOCAL DEALERS

Local dealers usually stock singles, sets, covers, accumulations, remainders—just about anything philatelic. If you're getting started, explain what you need. Don't be afraid to ask questions. Dealers are used to hearing questions and usually eager to share their knowledge. A good tip can save hours classifying varieties.

Most experienced collectors have had a dealer mentor, one who helped them get started, one upon whom they could rely on for advice, one who would keep an eye open for stamps to meet their highly specific needs.

Dealers network; they maintain contacts all over the nation, and often in foreign countries. If they don't have an item, they can usually obtain it or tell you where to find it. Shopping at a local dealer enables you to see stamps before buying, and to compare different types of albums, mounts, and supplies. And a good dealer is tuned in to everything philatelic going on in his or her area—meetings, clubs, shows, etc. Shopping at a local dealer also provides the opportunity to meet other collectors.

Sooner or later, you'll find one dealer who's been more helpful than the others, whom you enjoy talking to, and who seems to have just the right stamps for you. He's a valuable resource. Check the Yellow Pages for dealers in your area.

DIRECT MAIL

ADVERTISEMENTS AND PRICE LISTS. The more you learn about stamps, the more you'll discover that philately is largely an enterprise of specialists, both dealers and collectors. A single dealer—even the largest—just can't stock everything, either stamps or supplies. Fortunately, you can order just about anything by mail: individual stamps, sets, mixtures, job lots, covers, supplies, books, you name it. Some stamp dealers offer a selective new-issue service, which is useful for the topicalist who is not interested in all new issues of a country. Many dealers will send price lists upon request. Philatelic periodicals contain hundreds of display and classified ads. Most direct mail dealers are members of the American Philatelic Society (APS) or the American Stamp Dealers Association (ASDA) and subscribe to those organizations' codes of ethics. Look for their membership logos in ads.

APPROVALS. The term "approvals" refers to selections of stamps sent by mail for purchase subject to the buyer's approval. You look selections over (the time allotted is usually ten to fifteen days), pay for those you keep (there is no obligation to keep any), and return the rest. An initial selection usually amounts to ten dollars or less. The value of subsequent selections increases as you establish credit-worthiness. Most approval dealers offer a discount if you purchase the entire selection. In addition, some approval dealers allow you to earn credits (similar to frequent flier miles) toward future purchases. The first selection includes a questionnaire on which to indicate collecting preferences so that future selections can be oriented toward your interests. You'll continue to receive additional selections automatically until you notify the approval company to stop sending them. The mention of approvals almost invariably brings a smile of fond recollection to even the most seasoned philatelist's face. Countless numbers of collectors were introduced to the hobby through approvals. Philatelic periodicals contain advertisements for approval dealers.

TRADING. Look in the classified section of philatelic periodicals for collectors interested in trading.

Trading for cheap stamps is usually based on a stamp-for-stamp basis; new issues, on a face-value-for-face-value basis; and expensive, older stamps, on a catalogue-value-for-catalogue-value basis. Any equitable, mutually agreeable basis is okay. Many collectors enjoy the personal, one-on-one interaction with trading partners, especially those in foreign countries. You'd be surprised how many foreigners are interested in obtaining U.S. stamps, especially collectors in areas formerly behind the Iron Curtain.

MASS-MARKETED PHILATELIC COLLECTIBLES. As a rule, collectors rarely recoup their investment in mass-marketed philatelic collectibles—the type advertised with sugary buzz words such as "officially authorized," "limited edition," "certificate of authenticity"—and often get no more than a small fraction of the original purchase price. There is no secondary market for these products, and stamp dealers won't spend money on inventory they can't sell. Their customers prefer real stamps, not specially created collectibles. That's not an aesthetic or moral judgment, just a financial fact. Ask a dealer or fellow collector what has merit and you'll quickly learn what to avoid.

Another caveat: be suspicious of unsolicited direct mail offers promising huge investment gains in a short period of time. In some cases, "investors" receive off-grade stamps at inflated prices. In other cases, investors are made privy to "inside information" that when made public will cause the "hot property" to double or triple in short order. Trouble is, real philatelists couldn't care less about the "hot property," and when the inside information's made public, they yawn. Before buying any stamp for investment, check with dealers to find out if there's a secondary market for it.

AUCTIONS

Stamp auctions are an excellent source of material ranging from scarce individual stamps to collection remainders and bulk lots. Stamp auctions range from small local club operations to multimillion-dollar affairs. Regardless of their size, the idea is the same: to sell lots to the highest bidder. All stamp auctions publish catalogues containing descriptions including catalogue number, condition, and price (either catalogue price, estimated cash value, or reserve price). The figure is usually only for reference; bidders may bid as much or as little as they please. Most auction catalogues are illustrated, some with photographs of every lot, but most with only the best or most valuable lots. Check philatelic periodicals for announcements of forthcoming auctions.

You can bid in person, by mail, or through an agent. Floor bidders (in-person bidders) use a variety of strategies. There are too many to go into here; you'll quickly pick up on them if you decide to attend auctions. However, one strategy is worth mentioning. All experienced bidders follow it religiously: establish your maximum for each lot in advance and don't waver from it. The greatest mistake newcomers make is to fantasize about how little they expect to pay for a lot rather than to fix a maximum price for it. Then they get caught up in the frenzy of bidding and end up paying more than they should have. Establish your limit in advance. When you hit that limit, drop out. No exceptions. There will always be more stamps.

Most auctions add a 10 percent (in some cases 15 percent) buyer's fee to lots at settlement, so factor that into your maximum bid. A few charge no buyer's fee, but they're the exception rather than the rule. Most publish prices realized after each sale, which are useful for estimating bids in future auctions.

Read carefully the terms and conditions in each auction catalogue before bidding. They're very specific and vary from auction to auction. All state that placing a bid constitutes a contract. If your bid's successful, you've bought the lot, and lots are generally not returnable (except for cause). You may, at the time of sale, request that a lot be submitted for expert certificate, in which case the transaction will not be final until the certificate comes back, usually in six to eight weeks. If the stamp or cover comes back with a good (genuine and as described) certificate, you've bought the lot. If the stamp or cover comes back with a bad certificate (not genuine or not as described), then the auctioneer takes it back. It is customary for the auctioneer to pay the cost of a bad certificate, and for the buyer to pay the cost of a good certificate.

You may also bid by mail. Auction catalogues contain mail bid sheets. New bidders are required to provide references (society memberships or stamp dealer/financial references) and are usually asked to put down a good-faith deposit, typically 25 percent of the sum of the bids. Most auctions—but not all—buy lots for mail bidders at one bid over the highest floor bid, using a mail bidder's maximum bid only if necessary. Most auctions allow "either/or" bidding, which means you can bid on several similar lots but buy only one. Most auctions allow you to place a maximum on the total amount you want to spend. Once you've reached your maximum, the auctioneer stops executing your bids. Most bid sheets contain a box which, when checked, authorizes the auction house to increase your bids by a stated percentage, typically 10 percent or 20 percent. Avoid this. Let your basic bid stand as your maximum bid.

CAUTION: Check your bid sheet carefully before mailing it to make sure the lot numbers you've listed are correct. If you intend to bid $100 on Lot No. 454 but list Lot No. 545 by mistake, you'll be held to it. And it won't do any good to argue about it. And if you choose not to honor the bid, forget about bidding anywhere else. Dealers share deadbeat information.

Dealers and sharpshooters—individuals who

attend auctions for no other purpose than to pick off bargains—bid at most auctions and jump on bargains instantly. They provide the floor beneath which prices do not fall. If you're lucky, you can sometimes purchase a lot for one bid over a dealer's (think of it as cost plus). But don't expect to get a rare or superb stamp cheaply. These stamps routinely sell for multiples of catalogue or estimated cash value.

Get your feet wet at a small local auction or by mail with some inexpensive lots.

TIP: Pros usually avoid bidding on the first of several similar lots. The most eager bidder usually buys the first one, and the price of successive identical lots usually falls as each buyer in turn obtains a copy.

Mail bid sales are similar to auctions except that bidding is done exclusively by mail. Mail bid sales differ from auctions in one important respect: expect to pay the full amount of your bid, unless the terms and conditions indicate otherwise. So consider carefully your maximum bid on each lot. Mail bid sales usually do not charge a buyer's fee, which simplifies bidding.

STAMP CLUBS

Most stamp clubs permit members to bring stamps to meetings to trade or sell. Stamp clubs also provide a means of networking with fellow collectors and tapping into a tremendous pool of knowledge and experience.

Clubs typically meet once or twice a month. Large metropolitan areas often support several clubs, and collectors who just can't get enough of stamps belong to as many they have time and energy for. Dues are usually nominal, only a few dollars a year. Ask a local dealer to put you in touch with club representatives. Also, the APS provides its members with a handbook that lists more than 750 local clubs across America. Check the the resource guide for its address.

Some clubs meet in members' homes, but most

use church, school, or other public meeting rooms. Meetings often begin with a short business meeting (announcements, discussion of dues, etc., usually not longer than ten to fifteen minutes) followed by a program or slide show presented by a member or guest speaker. The program is usually followed by a general session in which members discuss stamps, compare collections, catch up on the latest news, and buy, sell, and trade stamps. Clubs often hold auctions, with a portion (or sometimes all) of the proceeds going to the club treasury, typically to purchase catalogues or benefit members in some other way.

No matter what your level of experience, membership in a local club will increase your knowledge of stamps and enrich your enjoyment of the hobby.

PHILATELIC SOCIETIES

Many philatelic societies make stamps available to members through sales divisions. Philatelic societies, as opposed to stamp clubs, tend to be national in nature, drawing on membership from all parts of the country. Rather than frequent meetings, societies tend to hold annual conventions—usually in conjunction with a stamp show—which rotate from city to city. Societies tend to be highly specialized in nature, such as the American First Day Cover Society (AFDCS) or the American Topical Association (ATA). The exception is the American Philatelic Society (APS), which is a general organization.

The APS has so much to offer that it is worth discussing in detail. The APS is a nonprofit organization founded in 1886, whose membership stands at about 55,000. The value of the APS lies is the abundance of resources it puts at a member's fingertips. The APS publishes an abundantly illustrated, slick-paper monthly journal, the *American Philatelist*, which alone is worth the society's nominal annual dues. Members also receive a services handbook and a dealer directory and are entitled to a discount on books published by the APS. And the

APS offers a stamp insurance plan designed specifi- cally for collectors, one that is less costly and more comprehensive than those available from standard casualty companies.

Upon request, members may obtain circuit books from the APS sales division by mail. Circuit books (they're actually booklets) contain selections of stamps for sale by other members. Members wishing to sell stamps obtain empty circuit books from the APS sales division, fill them, and return them to the sales division, which checks the stamps for accuracy and pricing, then enters the books into its inventory for dispatch to member requestees. Recipients make selections (they may purchase as many or as few items as they wish), send payment to the APS, and forward the books to the next collec- tor on the list enclosed with the selection—hence the name circuit books. The last collector on the circuit returns the books to the APS. Each recipient pays the cost of postage to forward the books to the next member on the circuit. Circuit books provide access to a wide range of reasonably priced stamps. The service is especially useful to collectors living in areas with no dealers nearby.

APS members are entitled to borrow books from the American Philatelic Research Library (APRL), one of the largest libraries in the world specifically dedicated to philately. The APRL contains two lin- ear miles of shelf space housing tens of thousands of books and periodicals devoted to philately. Most of its book loans are made by mail, to members all over America. For those living nearby, the library is located at 100 Oakwood Avenue in State College, Pennsylvania, and is open to the public.

APS members are also entitled to use the services of the American Philatelic Expertizing Service. (More about expertizing in the chapter on "Fakes and Forgeries.") Anyone may submit stamps to the American Philatelic Expertizing Service; however, APS members receive a substantial discount.

The APS also offers a summer seminar program that includes classes on a range of topics, such as fakes and forgeries; stamp technology; buying and selling; and computers in philately.

Dozens of other societies exist, one for nearly every specialty, and far too many to discuss individually here. Some are large, others small. Most publish journals or newsletters, the size, frequency, and production values of which vary with the size and budget of the organization. Many publish quarterly, a few more often. Dues are usually nominal. Some offer circuit books; others do not.

In summary, stamp societies offer access to stamps, highly detailed publications, and a network of kindred spirits whose reservoir of knowledge is both deep and wide. There is no better way to keep abreast of the latest developments within a specialty.

STAMP SHOWS

Stamp shows generally consist of two elements: a dealer bourse and an exhibition of stamps. Shows range in size from small local affairs with half a dozen dealers to national and international shows featuring hundreds of frames of exhibits and hundreds of dealers.

The bourse section of a show consists of dealers offering their wares from tables or booths. The larger the show, the more dealers. Dealers from all over the world take booths at giant international shows. Stamps shows, regardless of their size, con-

Collectors browsing at a stamp show bourse.

centrate dealers into a single location, affording the opportunity to view and buy a range of material otherwise unavailable in one place. There's no better place to comparison-shop.

One of the most popular attractions at national and international shows is foreign post office booths offering their latest stamps at face value. Some even premiere new stamps at shows and have stamp designers available to autograph first day covers. Local shows are usually held annually, although it's not uncommon for a large metropolitan area to host a number of shows sponsored by different groups during the course of a year. Dealer bourses (usually one-day affairs without exhibits) are common in large cities and are typically held once or twice a month.

The exhibition section of a show features exhibits prepared by collectors and displayed in rows of large frames. The U.S. Postal Service sometimes displays an exhibit of proofs, uncut press sheets, and other material from its archives that's seldom seen by the public. On occasion, the Bureau of Engraving and Printing brings a small intaglio press (known as a spider press) and demonstrates the intaglio printing process by hand-pulling (printing) souvenir cards, which are for sale to visitors. Attending a national or international show is like going to Disneyland. You leave disappointed that you had not allowed more time to see and do things.

Exhibits are especially worthwhile for the novice. Nothing gives one a better feel for philately than viewing exhibits and seeing how others have approached collecting. In addition, large shows often feature lectures, programs, and seminars, usually at no cost, which are valuable learning tools. There is no better place to meet fellow collectors, ask questions, share information, view, and learn.

In summary, stamp shows concentrate dealers, collectors, and exhibits in one place, offering an unequaled opportunity to buy stamps, to see how others are approaching the philately, and to learn.

FORMING A COLLECTION

Most collectors get their feet wet with a basic starter album, a pair of tongs, some hinges, and a few packets of stamps or some kiloware. When getting started, it's easy to go off in a hundred directions and buy every stamp that comes along. This can get expensive, so it's wise to think about a goal, or at least parameters, and become selective. Most collectors, as they mature, graduate from quantity to quality, from the general to the specific.

Soon after becoming interested in stamps, collectors gravitate toward either mint or used stamps. Those who prefer mint stamps feel that cancellations intrude on a stamp's design and distract from its beauty, and that soaking a stamp off paper diminishes its freshness. Those who prefer used stamps usually argue that a stamp is not really a stamp until it's gone through the mail, been canceled, and served its intended purpose. You might as well argue about which is better, chocolate or vanilla. As a practical matter, country collectors usually obtain mint stamps as far back as they can, then fill in with used stamps. The dividing line for United States stamps is usually around the years 1890 or 1900.

GENERAL COLLECTING

There was a time—now long past—when all the different stamps of the world would fit in a single album, and collectors tried to obtain an example of each. They were known as general collectors. Today it requires more than forty albums, each four to five inches thick, to accommodate all the stamps of the world, which number several hundred thousand. The cost of these albums alone is nearly $2,000. And the annual cost to acquire all the new issues of the world—and there are thousands—is staggering, roughly $7,500 to $10,000. Today, general collectors rarely collect with an eye toward completion. Instead, they enjoy the challenge of seeing how many different stamps they can acquire.

TIP: If you decide to pursue general collecting, buy the largest loose-leaf general album you can afford and add supplements and blank pages as needed.

A new breed of generalists collect just those sets and singles that catch their eye, stamps that may have no logical relationship to one another but intrigue them nevertheless. This form of limited general collecting is becoming more popular all the time. One fellow calls his general collection simply "personal favorites."

COUNTRY COLLECTING

Country collecting, i.e., collecting the stamps of a given nation, is the most popular method of collecting in the world. Collectors of each nation tend to collect the stamps of their country: Americans collect U.S. stamps; Germans collect German stamps; Chinese collect Chinese stamps. Americans also enjoy collecting foreign stamps, most often from the nations of their ethnic heritage. The images on stamps from our ancestral lands have a powerful effect; holding the stamps and pondering the images puts us directly in touch with our ethnic history and our roots.

Most country collectors house their collections

in specialty albums, which can be purchased from a stamp dealer or mail order supply dealer. A great variety of country albums exist, ranging in price from $40 or $50 to many hundreds of dollars, depending on the size of the country's output, the album's degree of comprehensiveness, and the quality of the album.

TOPICAL COLLECTING

Topical collecting is popular because it's so simple and so much fun. The idea is to acquire as many different stamps as possible illustrating a topic of interest. Among the more popular topics are dogs, cats, birds, flowers, airplanes, trains, ships, fine art, music, aerospace, sports, medicine, chess, and religion. Even Elvis and Marilyn Monroe are collected. The choices are limited only by one's imagination.

Topics need not be limited to the subject of a stamp. Czeslaw Slania, one of the world's most talented and prolific stamp engravers, has more than a thousand stamps to his credit, all incredibly detailed, all miniature masterpieces. A growing number of collectors specialize in acquiring just stamps engraved by this master.

There was once a woman who collected only stamps printed in green. Another man limited his collection exclusively to stamps bearing the numeral 10. And at least one collector judiciously acquires stamps that were never stamps, i.e., artists' conceptions of stamps used in advertising and promotion. He has amassed hundreds of examples, which when displayed together are indeed striking, and evidence of how pervasive, if only subliminally, postage stamps are in our lives and culture.

Washington Press publishes a variety of high-quality pages for topicals under the brand name White Ace. The American Topical Association (ATA), one of the largest philatelic societies in the world, offers much to the topicalist, including its journal *Topical Time*, a marvelous variety of handbooks devoted to specific topics, and a members' sales circuit. Check the resource guide for its address.

POSTAL HISTORY

Strictly speaking, postal history is the study and collection of stamps, covers, or other materials relating to the operation or evolution of a postal system or element of a postal system. Lately, the term "postal history" is being used more loosely to describe covers that illustrate or relate to some historical epoch, such as World War II. Postal history collections are essentially stories told and illustrated through the use of covers and stamps.

Postal history knows no national boundaries, and any facet of the development of the delivery of mail can be collected and studied, broad or narrow: a national system, state system, or even local system, for example, the Confederate postal system, the pony express, or V-mail developed during World War II. The most trying times in human history often provide the most fertile ground for the postal history collector.

Postal history can be as expensive or inexpensive as one wants to make it. It is not uncommon to see

This cover bears stamps of both Costa Rica and the United States as well as a censor tape. A postal history specialist could explain why this was necessary.

valuable and remarkable collections assembled from seemingly unremarkable parts. Knowledge enables the postal history collector to do this. Postal history collectors love to trade stories about the valuable covers they've found in dealers' bargain boxes, covers passed over by others because no one recognized their significance. Finding treasure is part of the appeal of postal history.

Some contend that every cover tells a story, if only one inquires deeply enough. And it's true. That's what postal history is all about.

OTHER METHODS OF COLLECTING

ACCUMULATING AND HOARDING. Not all stamp collectors are organized or focused. The hobby is home to many "hoarders" and "accumulators" who buy, trade, or otherwise try to get as many stamps as they can. Some are treasure hunters; others just love to accumulate stamps and covers for no particular reason.

Some accumulators buy job lots (large, often disorganized accumulations), remainders, and mixtures from dealers, estates, and auctions hoping to find something valuable that someone else overlooked or didn't have sufficient knowledge to recognize. Others search lots and mixtures, remove what they want, then sell or trade the balance (often for a profit) to offset the cost of what they've kept. Still others bring boxes and cartons home and put them in closets or basements, where they gather dust for years. The dyed-in-the-wool hoarder seems to get more of a kick out of acquiring stamps than doing anything with them.

Some enterprising individuals arrange to get empty envelopes from utility companies or other high-volume mail sources and sift through them looking for oddities and unusual items, which either interest them and fit in their collections, or which they can sell. This low-cost method of collecting requires no special tools except access to raw material, a willingness to sort through it, and a knowledge of what to look for.

CASUAL COLLECTING. According to the U.S. Postal Service, many Americans save (rather than collect) stamps; that is to say, they tuck away examples of only those stamps that appeal to them, such as depictions of Elvis or Marilyn Monroe. They're neither aware of nor participate in organized philately. They don't own albums, tongs, or accessories. They retain only stamps they like with no thought to forming a collection. According to the postal service, there are more than 20 million casual collectors in America.

INVESTING. Investors buy stamps with an eye toward profit (building a portfolio) rather than aesthetics or completion. They often store their acquisitions in a safe-deposit box. At least one firm, USID Inc., publishes a series of investor-oriented books, *The StampFinder Stamp Selection Guides*, which contain price performance information on stamps of the United States and Canada; Mexico and South America; Germany and the German Area; British Commonwealth; and the Far East. Refer to the bibliography. In addition, several firms publish computer software for tracking inventory and updating value. They advertise in philatelic periodicals.

UNITED STATES

Collecting U.S. stamps is the most popular specialty in America, and there are so many subspecialties that they could easily fill a book by themselves. I touch on the basics in the next chapter.

In summary, collect what you enjoy; that's what it's all about. Tailor your collection to fit your interests and your budget.

COLLECTING U.S. STAMPS

Collecting United States stamps is by far the most popular choice in America. The majority of U.S. collectors approach the hobby in one of several ways: collecting singles, plate blocks, PNCs, or first day covers, or specializing in an individual stamp or series.

GENERAL U.S. COLLECTING

Collecting single copies of stamps (as opposed to blocks or panes) is the most economical and least complex way of collecting U.S. stamps. Most collectors try to obtain an example of every U.S. postage stamp ever issued, beginning with the latest stamps available at the post office and working backward, crossing the bridges of expensive items as they come to them. Assembling a collection of twentieth-century stamps is not particularly difficult, although it is more costly to collect mint stamps than used stamps. Still, you need not be wealthy to form such a collection. Collecting nineteenth-century stamps is a different story. Only the most dedicated collector with unlimited funds stands a chance of completing a mint collection of nineteenth-century stamps. It is much less costly and far more realistic to collect used stamps, which is what most collectors, even serious ones, usually do. Of course, you can fill spaces of the less expensive nineteenth-century stamps with mint copies if you choose, and many do. As a practical matter, most U.S. collections contain mint examples of twentieth-century issues and used examples of nineteenth-century issues.

A few collectors limit their scope to commemorative stamps, which pretty much eliminates nineteenth-century issues.

TIP: Limit your purchases of new issues at the post office to exactly what you need for your collection. Avoid buying duplicates as an investment; they usually do not rise in value. And if you want to get the most from your collecting budget, collect singles, not multiples such as blocks and panes.

The market offers a tremendous variety of U.S. albums, ranging from solid, no-frills basics to magnificent, top-of-the-line hingeless albums. Check with your local dealer or with a mail order supply firm.

PLATE BLOCKS

Plate block collecting has been popular for decades. A plate block consists of four or more stamps on whose selvage appears a printing plate number or numbers. Every printing plate used for stamps is assigned a plate number for security purposes. Plates are logged on press and a record kept of every impression made from each plate. Thousands of sheets are printed from each plate, and all

Plate block of 6 at left; plate block of 4 at right.

printed from a given plate bear the same plate number. Printing a large or extended issue requires dozens and sometimes even hundreds of plates, each of which has its own plate number.

Before the late 1960s, most twentieth-century plate blocks consisted of either four or six stamps, depending on the placement of the plate number in the selvage. Plate numbers appearing in the corner of a pane are collected in blocks of four. Plate numbers appearing elsewhere on the selvage are collected in blocks of six (or more, depending on the number of plate numbers) with the plate number(s) appearing on the center piece (or pieces) of selvage for aesthetic balance. It is crucial that the plate number(s) appear on the center selvage tab(s) of these issues rather than to the left or right of center. If the plate number(s) do not appear on the center tab(s), the block is not a plate block and not worth the premium a plate block commands, which can be as much as ten times or more the value of the stamps as individual items.

This plate block contains five numbers and requires ten stamps.

With the advent of multicolor printing, the postal service began spreading numbers (one for each plate employed in the color printing process) up and down the selvage. Plate blocks grew as large as eight, ten, even twelve stamps or more. Lately, however, the postal service has condensed the placement of plate numbers to one or two corner selvage tabs. Now nearly all plate blocks consist of four stamps. U.S. specialized catalogues list the precise number of stamps necessary for each plate block.

Most plate block collectors try to get a plate block of each stamp. However, plate blocks simply do not exist for many nineteenth-century stamps, so absolute completion is impossible. Those nineteenth-century plate blocks that do exist are scarce and expensive, usually beginning in the low thousands and running as high as $150,000 or more. As a practical matter, most plate block collectors content themselves with working their way back as far as they can go.

The *Durland Standard Plate Number Catalog*, published by the Bureau Issues Association, contains a comprehensive listing of U.S. plate numbers and positions, some of which are rare and expensive.

PLATE NUMBER COILS

Since 1981, plate numbers have also appeared on coil stamps, giving rise to one of the most popular specialties in U.S. philately: plate number coil (PNC) collecting. Before 1981, coil plate numbers were trimmed off in the finishing process as the stamps were slit apart and rolled into coils.

Next time you buy a roll of stamps, unwind it slowly, keeping an eye toward the bottom of the stamps. Soon you'll encounter a stamp with a tiny plate number (or numbers, in the case of multicolored stamps) underneath the design. You will have found a PNC. Plate numbers appear at various intervals (typically, every 24 or 52 stamps), depending on the printing plate used, so those of some issues are more abundant than others. PNCs are collected in strips, usually of three or five stamps, with the plate number on the center stamp. The number *must* be on the center stamp or it is not a collectible strip. Some collectors try to acquire every number used to print a given issue, typically anywhere from one or two plates up to a maximum of perhaps twenty-five. Scarce PNC numbers can

Contemporary cover with PNC single. Note the plate number at the bottom of the stamp.

run into hundreds of dollars. Fortunately, there are not many.

PNC collectors look for covers bearing stamps with plate numbers, especially scarce numbers. Columns in philatelic periodicals keep collectors up-to-date on scarce numbers. Every household and business in America receive a steady supply of bulk mail containing coil stamps. Keep your eyes open for covers with PNCs. Finding a scarce number is like hitting a mini-lottery.

PNC collecting is so popular because it's new, sufficiently challenging to make it interesting, yet not so complex or expensive that completion is impossible. The essential reference for PNC collectors is *Linn's Plate Number Coil Handbook* by Ken Lawrence.

FIRST DAY COVERS

First-day covers (FDCs) contain stamps canceled on the first day they were available for public sale. Until the twentieth century, the postal service seldom announced an official first day of sale for new stamps. It just shipped stamps to post offices, which placed them on sale as they saw fit. Today, however, the USPS announces an official first day of issue for each new stamp. Usually (but not always) a new stamp is placed on sale only in a single city (known as the official city) on its first day of issue.

The stamp goes on sale nationwide the following day. Most first day covers are postmarked in the official city with a special cancel containing the words "First Day of Issue."

You can send in your own covers for first day cancellation; however, most FDC collectors subscribe to a new-issue service to avoid the inconvenience of preparing and mailing their own covers and to ensure that they don't miss an issue. Ordering from a service also eliminates the risk of having a cover damaged or overcanceled on its journey through the mail stream.

Some collectors specialize. They try to obtain every cachet ever produced by a particular cachet maker, especially those of the early cachet makers, each of which has its own special charm. Others concentrate on a specific stamp, such as the statehood stamp of their home state, and try to collect every different cachet produced for it—and there can be dozens and dozens. Still others prefer hand-colored or hand-painted cachets, which are usually done in very limited quantities (typically 10 to 75) and tend to hold their value more than mass-produced cachets. Cachet artists use watercolor, acrylic, colored pencil, and occasionally other media to execute their designs. The results are vivid and spectacular, much more eye-arresting than mass-produced covers. Purists eschew add-ons—i.e., cachets painted on older FDCs years after the cover was issued—and insist on covers painted contemporaneously with the stamp. Prices for hand-painted covers by recognized FDC artists such as Dorothy Knapp (a pioneer in the hand-painted cachet field) can run into hundreds of dollars.Hand painted new issues are generally priced from $10 to $75.

Hand-colored cachets differ from hand-painted cachets in that the outline of a design is first printed on a cover; then areas within the design are colored by hand. Hand-colored cachets are usually issued in larger editions, which can run as high as several hundred, and typically sell for less than hand-painted cachets.

FDC bearing both official and unofficial cancels.

The postal service allows a grace period (usually thirty days) after a stamp is issued, during which time one can obtain a first day cancellation. This means that not all FDCs are actually canceled on their first day of issue, a fact that doesn't bother most collectors. However, purists insist on *actual* first day cancellations. To get them, they buy newly issued stamps at the official first day city, prepare covers, then drive to post offices in other towns and cities to have them canceled, usually by hand cancel. Since the grace period applies only to the official city, covers bearing postmarks from any other place dated on the first day of issue must, by necessity, have been canceled on that day only, and are first day covers in the truest sense of the word. Such FDCs are known as unofficial first day covers. Ironically, "unofficial" covers are more indisputably genuine than "official" covers.

FDC collectors prefer cacheted covers; however, few cachet makers operated before 1935, so cacheted covers prior to this date are the exception rather than the rule, and worth a premium. Collectors generally insist that FDCs produced after 1935 have cachets. Those FDCs produced after 1935 without cachets generally have little value, unless the stamp itself is valuable. Collectors also prefer unaddressed FDCs where possible, but unaddressed FDCs are seldom available on covers produced before 1945. Unaddressed FDCs produced before 1945 sell for a premium because they are so scarce. Unaddressed FDCs produced after 1945 are abundant. Addressed covers produced after 1945 are unsalable. You can buy post-1945 FDCs from stamp dealers in assortments of 100 or more at very reasonable prices.

The *Scott U.S. First Day Cover Catalogue and Checklist* is an excellent general catalogue that lists and prices all FDCs, including premiums applicable to cachets of the major cachet producers. The *Planty Photo Encyclopedia of Cacheted First Day Covers* zeroes in on the classic period 1901 through 1939, illustrating and pricing every known cachet from the period, many of which are worth big bucks. It's a must for the serious collector.

Before the year 1920, the postal service made no special effort to announce issue dates for definitive stamps, and few commemoratives existed. Even after it began announcing dates of issue, most collectors remained uninterested in obtaining FDCs. Consequently, few first day covers prior to 1920 exist. Those that do are generally worth hundreds or even thousands of dollars. Early first day covers do not bear the slogan cancel "First Day of Issue," and they lack cachets. The date on the postmark is the only clue. Treasures wait to be discovered, if you know what to look for and are willing to take the time to check.

First day covers for stamps issued before 1900 are rare. So collectors go after EKU (earliest known use) covers, i.e., covers postmarked as close to the first day of issue as possible. Sometimes the earliest known use is only a few days after the actual issue date of the stamp; other times its weeks or months later. Nineteenth-century EKU covers are rare; often no more than a single example per issue exists. Prices generally start in the low thousands and climb to more than $125,000.

Today, stamps are occasionally sold and used before they are supposed to be, giving rise to the modern EKU cover, i.e., earliest known use before the official first day of issue. Early use of modern stamps occurs because post offices receive supplies of stamps well in advance of their issue date. With so many new stamps constantly arriving, clerks cannot always keep track of which is supposed to be issued when, especially during hectic periods such as Christmas. Most modern EKUs are discovered by collectors checking dates on incoming mail. The most fertile ground for discovering EKU covers is in business correspondence received by large-volume mail recipients such as utility and insurance companies. Although not worth much, modern EKUs are avidly collected by specialists. Information about forthcoming and recently issued stamps appears in all the philatelic weeklies.

Membership in the American First Day Cover Society (AFDCS) is recommended for anyone seriously interested in first day covers. The AFDCS (see resource guide) publishes a thick journal eight times a year. It's loaded with articles devoted to FDC collecting.

SINGLE STAMP OR SERIES

Some collectors are fascinated by a single series, such the 1869 pictorials, the Washington-Franklin series, or the Liberty series, and limit their collections to stamps of the series. Others narrow their focus even further, concentrating on a single stamp. They study the stamp in infinite detail, collect all varieties, including plate flaws, color shades, and paper and gum varieties. Specializing in a single stamp or single series is nothing new. Before commemoratives existed, serious philatelists collected, studied, and documented the definitive stamps of their era, stamps that today are classics. It is the dream of every serious philatelist to build a collection of one of the classic issues, but it's usually beyond an individual's financial resources. However, you can still derive the same sense of challenge and discovery by specializing in modern issues, such as definitive stamps. A small but growing number of collectors are beginning to study them because the raw material is readily available and can often be had for the asking. The quest is

Examples of the 1954 Liberty definitive series.

usually more time-intensive than cash-intensive.

Students of single stamps and single series immerse themselves in an issue. They find the challenge of discovery more satisfying than just acquiring new issues. They search out and assemble collections of shades, printing and perforation varieties, gum varieties, examples on cover illustrating rates and usages, and even counterfeits.

The Liberty series of 1954 is a good example. Although at first glance it appears very straightforward (27 sheet stamps, 8 coil stamps, 2 booklet panes), specialists have discovered a myriad of collectible varieties: wet printings and dry printings; large-hole coils and small-hole coils; tagged and untagged varieties, some of which are valuable. There even exists two values counterfeited by North Korea to mail propaganda to South Korea. Liberty series specialists have discovered these varieties through research and study, often acquiring examples for next to nothing because the Liberty series is so recent no one pays much attention to it. The great rarities of the Liberty series are just as elusive as some classic rarities. It would be hard to put a price on any of the better Liberty specialized collections because none has come to market, but the best among them would easily fetch thousands of dollars. Single stamp and single series specialization yields great dividends, in terms of both enjoyment and profit.

OTHER SPECIALTIES

STATE POSTMARKS. Some collectors try to get a postmark from every city in their state. The challenge arises in finding the DPOs (discontinued post offices), many of which were closed decades ago. Collectors of state postmarks inevitably become immersed in the history of their state, increasing their knowledge and understanding of the area in which they live. Collectors insist on complete covers. Postmarks cut from the covers, no matter how neatly, are worth little. Books on state post offices exist for many states.

PRECANCELS. Precancels bearing city and state overprints are collected in much the same fashion as postmarks of states, except that precancels are almost always collected off cover and mounted on album pages. Precancel collecting is generally less expensive than cover collecting. Most examples can be purchased for less than half a dollar. Town collectors try to obtain one precancel from each town that issued them; town and type collectors try to obtain one precancel of each type from each town (towns often make use of several different precanceling devices over the course of the years). Bureau precancel collectors attempt to get a copy of every precancel printed by the Bureau of Engraving and Printing. Contact the Precancel Stamp Society (see resource guide) for more information on this specialty.

DUCK STAMPS. Philatelists, hunters, and conservationists alike enjoy collecting the large, colorful waterfowl hunting stamps issued by the Department of the Interior (known as federal duck stamps). The first was issued in 1934. Most catalogues list federal duck stamps. States began issuing

State duck stamp top; federal duck stamp at bottom.

duck stamps in the early 1970s. Few people collect issues of all states; most prefer to concentrate on those of their state.

ERRORS. More and more collectors are becoming intrigued by major errors and EFOs. Errors tend to be more expensive than other kinds of stamps because they exist in small quantities; however, there are fewer to collect and they hold their value well.

B-O-B. Back-of-the-book collecting appeals to those who prefer smaller, generally finite issues such as airmails, special deliveries, and postage dues, all of which the United States no longer issues. B-O-B includes revenues and other issues that appear after listings for definitives and commemoratives in the catalogue, hence the name back-of-the-book.

These are just a few examples of what U.S. collecting has to offer. The opportunities are limitless.

RARE STAMPS

The British Guiana one-cent magenta and the U.S. inverted Jenny, the stamp with the upside-down airplane, are two of the most famous and most valuable stamps in the world. A schoolboy discovered one; a clerk discovered the other on his way to work.

THE WORLD'S RAREST STAMP

The British Guiana one-cent magenta is often referred to as the world's rarest stamp or the world's most valuable stamp. Although only a single copy is known to exist, the one-cent magenta cannot accurately be described as the world's rarest stamp because quite a few other stamps exist of which only a single copy is known. It is arguably the world's most expensive stamp because no single stamp off cover has ever sold for as much—$935,000 in 1980. The unique Alexandria, Virginia, postmaster's provisional issued in 1846, known as the Blue Boy by virtue of being printed on blue paper, reportedly sold by private treaty for $1 million in 1981. However, the Blue Boy was on cover, and rare stamps on cover are generally regarded as more valuable than those off cover. It is argued that had the Blue Boy not been on cover, it would have sold for less. So in the minds of most, the one-cent magenta is still the

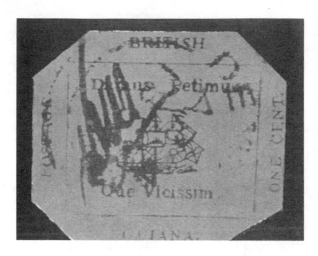

The British Guiana one-cent magenta.

world's single most valuable stamp. And there is no question that the British Guiana one-cent magenta is the world's best-known rarity.

The one-cent magenta, so called because it is printed on a deep wine-red paper, is not a particularly attractive stamp but a crude attempt by a local printer to make something that would pass for a postage stamp. In 1856, when the one-cent magenta was printed, British Guiana was a remote outpost of the British Empire located north of Brazil in South America, and its printing facilities were rudimentary. The stamp's central feature is a stock printer's cut of a ship around which appear the name of the colony, the value of the stamp, and a Latin motto. Somewhere along the line, someone trimmed the corners off the stamp, giving it its trademark octagonal shape. Most would say the stamp is ugly. Perhaps young L. Vernon Vaughan, the boy who discovered it in 1863, thought so, too, which may have been the reason he decided to part with it for six shillings (about $1.50), or perhaps he thought a better copy might come along.

He sold it to N. R. McKinnon, who added it to his stamp collection. McKinnon kept it for several years, then sold it to Thomas Ridpath, a stamp dealer from Liverpool, England. Ridpath sold it to Count Philippe von Ferrari, who at the time was the world's most avid stamp collector. (More about Ferrari in the next chapter, "Famous Collectors.") Ferrari appreciated the one-cent magenta's rarity and did not quibble over the $700 or so it cost him—the exact figure is not clear. He kept it until his death in 1917.

By the time Ferrari's vast collection came on the market in the 1920s, knowledgeable collectors throughout the world had begun to appreciate the true rarity of the one-cent magenta. It was the one stamp necessary to complete King George V of Great Britain's collection of stamps of the British Empire. In addition to George V, Maurice Burrus, a Swiss tobacco magnate, and Arthur Hind, a wealthy American textile manufacturer, wanted the stamp and competed for it when Ferrari's collection appeared at auction. When the dust settled, Hind had outbid his rivals, securing the one-cent magenta for the then record price of $32,500.

Hind kept the stamp until he died in 1933, at which time it passed to his widow. She held it until 1940, then sold it by private treaty to a collector named Frederick T. Small for about $40,000. Small owned the stamp until 1970, when he offered it through Robert A. Siegel's Rarities of the World auction, where it sold for a record price of $280,000. The new owners, a syndicate of investors headed by Pennsylvania stamp dealer Irwin Weinberg, held the stamp until 1980, when it again appeared in Robert A. Siegel's annual Rarities of the World sale. Many felt the one-cent magenta would surpass the $1 million mark, especially in a boom market fueled by inflation. It came close. The bidding stopped at $850,000 ($935,000 including the 10 percent buyer's premium), just shy of $1 million. The anonymous buyer was later revealed to be John E. duPont.

THE INVERTED JENNY

On the morning of May 14, 1918, William T. Robey, a cashier at Hibbs and Company in Washington, D.C., stopped on his way to work to purchase some new bicolored 24-cent airmail stamps that were being placed on sale that day. The stamp featured a Curtiss Jenny biplane printed in blue surrounded by a carmine frame. Robey, an enthusiastic stamp collector, planned to use some of the new stamps on first flight covers that were to be carried to Philadelphia and New York via airplane the next day. He asked the clerk for a pane of one hundred, which the clerk pulled from his drawer and laid on the counter. When Robey saw that the airplane was upside down, his heart stood still. He quickly tendered payment, hoping the clerk would not notice the error, tucked the pane away, and hurried off to work. At work, he showed the odd-looking stamps to fellow employees, and during the course of the day shared the news via telephone with friends. The word spread like wildfire. Soon eager collectors hurried to post offices all over the city hoping to discover more inverts.

Having been alerted by the inadvertent remarks of error seekers, postal inspectors visited Robey at his office that afternoon, demanding to see the error pane. When Robey refused, they threatened to confiscate it. Robey stood his ground, and the postal inspectors finally left in a huff. After work,

The inverted Jenny.

Robey visited the office of Washington stamp dealer Hamilton F. Colman, where a group of collectors had gathered to see Robey's pane. Colman had earlier offered Robey $500 for it, but Robey declined. Robey asked the group what they thought the pane ought to be worth, but no one had a firm opinion. One fellow reminded Robey that stamps were printed in sheets of 400, then cut into panes of 100 for sale over the counter, so it was possible that more panes existed. The more that existed, the less Robey's pane would be worth. However, unbeknownst to Robey and his friends, the 24-cent airmail had been printed one sheet (one pane) of 100 at a time. Nor did they know that as soon as the government learned of the error, it had instructed clerks to check their stocks and remove any faulty panes. No more would be found, but Robey had no way of knowing that.

Postal inspectors visited Robey's apartment later the same evening, but he had not yet returned home. They waited outside for a while, then left. Robey, apparently fearing just such an eventuality, had ridden around on a streetcar after leaving Colman's office, waiting until after dark to come home. Robey and his wife spent an anxious night with the pane of inverted Jennies tucked under their mattress.

Again, the following day, a postal inspector visited Robey at work, insisting once more that he surrender the stamps. Robey again refused. Pressure from the postal inspectors together with the possibility that other panes might be discovered crystallized Robey's decision to sell the stamps as quickly as possible. He sent telegrams to several out-of-town dealers, among them Elliot Perry of Westfield, New Jersey, and Percy Mann of Philadelphia. Perry didn't have a feel for the value of the pane; Mann came to Washington, viewed the pane, and offered $10,000 for it, which Robey declined. Three days after he had discovered the pane, Robey decided to go to New York City and try his luck.

On May 17, Robey took a train to New York.

First he stopped at the office of Colonel Edward H. R. Green, the eccentric multimillionaire collector, but Green was out of town. Next he talked to dealers at Stanley Gibbons Ltd., and at Scott Stamp and Coin Company, and he talked to John Klemann of Nassau Stamp Company, but couldn't make a deal with any of them. None thought the stamps were worth anywhere near the $10,000 Mann had offered. Discouraged, Robey telephoned Mann from New York that night to tell him that no one had matched his offer, but that he had decided to keep the pane rather than sell it. However, Mann was not about to give up. He kept talking and finally persuaded Robey to stop in Philadelphia on his way to Washington the next day. After Robey arrived in Philadelphia, Mann introduced him to Eugene Klein, who was a well-known local dealer. Klein asked Robey to name his price. Robey replied that he'd have to get at least $15,000. Klein didn't object to the price, but wanted a twenty-four-hour option to buy the pane. Robey thought it over for a moment, then agreed. Klein would have until three o'clock the following day to buy the pane for $15,000.

Robey returned to Washington, perhaps sorry he had not asked for more money. It is reported that Hamilton Colman offered Robey $18,000 upon his return, but that Robey couldn't accept because of Klein's option. In any case, Klein telephoned the next day to exercise his option, requesting that Robey appear at his office in Philadelphia the following day to close the deal. The next morning Robey, accompanied by his father-in-law, boarded the train to Philadelphia with a shoe box clutched under his arm. The pane of inverted Jennies was inside. At Klein's office, Robey handed over the shoebox in return for a cashier's check for $15,000. Robey had made a $14,976 profit in less than a week.

Klein had used his twenty-four-hour option to arrange a sale for the invert pane with Colonel

Green, the same Colonel Green Robey had attempted to see on his trip to New York. Green, who had a special weakness for inverts, agreed to pay $20,000 for the pane, a quick $5,000 profit for Klein.

Klein also worked out an arrangement with Green to sell surplus copies of the invert, first for $250 each, which Klein split $225/$25 with Green, and later for $350 each, which he split $225/$125 with Green. Green suggested that Klein keep the extra $100 when the price rose to $350. With an income estimated at more than $2 million a year, Green apparently wasn't concerned with a few hundred dollars. Green kept the choice pieces: the center line block, the plate block of eight, an arrow block, and the lower left margin block. Klein sold a fair number of Green's surplus inverts, although at the time of Green's death in 1936, forty-one copies remained in the colonel's possession. When Green's four key pieces were auctioned, the plate block realized $27,000; the center line block, $22,000; the lower left corner block, $17,000; and the arrow block, which had been broken into pairs, $13,750—a total of $79,750, nearly four times the original cost to Green of the pane.

Those who bought the inverts early on got in on the ground floor. In the years that followed, prices rose whenever inverts came to market. A single copy sold in 1969 for $33,000. Eight years later the same stamp sold for $62,500. In 1978, the inverted Jenny broke the $100,000 mark for a single stamp. Less desirable copies sold for substantially less, as little as $65,000, still an enormous appreciation over their original cost. The stamp market exploded in the late 1970s, and with it the price of inverts. In 1982, at the peak of the market, a select copy realized $198,000 ($180,000 plus $18,000 buyer's premium) in Robert A. Siegel's Rarities of the World sale. Since then, prices for inverts have stabilized at a lower but still-stratospheric level of $100,000 to $125,000.

William T. Robey won the post office lottery. Over the decades, others have won the post office lottery, too. Everyone who buys stamps plays, and the payoff can be big, if you know what to look for. (More about that in the chapter on "Errors on Stamps.")

CHAPTER 9

_F_AMOUS COLLECTORS

Count Philippe von Ferrari is regarded as the greatest stamp collector who ever lived. Born in France in 1848 of wealthy parents, Ferrari was a sickly, fragile child. His mother introduced him to stamps when he was ten years old, hoping they would entertain him and take his mind off his troubles. The intricately printed bits of paper fascinated young Ferrari. Almost immediately, he decided that he would own a copy of every stamp ever issued, and he never wavered from that goal. By the time he was in his thirties, Ferrari had amassed the most complete collection then known. Along the way, he had inherited one of the greatest fortunes in Europe, which simplified the task. He spent millions of French francs on stamps, seeking out individual rarities as well as buying some of the finest collections in the world intact.

Philippe von Ferrari.

In 1878, Ferrari acquired the unique British Guiana one-cent magenta for approximately $700, a lot of money in those days. He acquired every rarity he encountered without hesitation, allowing his philatelic curator, Pierre Mahe, a budget of 50,000 francs per week to buy stamps. At one point, Ferrari's relatives, thinking he was crazy for "squandering" so much money on stamps, went to court to stop him. The judge decided that Ferrari's behavior might be eccentric but it was not insane. Ferrari zealously continued his quest for stamps until his death in 1917.

Ferrari never exhibited his collection or showed it to anyone except his philatelic curators. He bought and bought and bought, and salted his purchases away.

In all, Count Ferrari devoted fifty-six years of his life to collecting stamps. After his death, his magnificent collection was disbursed in a series of fourteen sales held between 1921 and 1925. The Ferrari auctions attracted bidders from all over the globe, either in person or represented by agent. The bidders constituted a veritable who's who of philately: Alfred Caspery, Maurice Burrus, King George V of Great Britain, Alfred Lichtenstein, and Arthur Hind. The combined sales yielded $1,428,000, an astronomical sum of money at the time.

King George V, who reigned from 1910 to 1936, was an avid collector and a philatelic scholar as well. Unlike Ferrari, George V did not attempt to obtain every stamp in the world. He specialized in stamps of the British Empire and formed a magnificent collection of stunning quality and comprehensiveness, which included proofs, specimens, and artwork—every conceivable item the resources of

King George V of Great Britain.

the monarchy could bring to bear on the quest. The king's collection lacked only one item for completion: the unique British Guiana one-cent magenta, which came to market during the series of Ferrari auctions. George V sent an agent to bid on the stamp, but the extravagant and boorish American textile manufacturer Arthur Hind outbid him. Hind paid $32,500 for the one-cent magenta, the highest price ever paid for a single postage stamp at the time. It's been rumored—but never confirmed—that Hind offered the rarity to George V as a gift, but the king declined. Later, during a visit to Buckingham Palace at the invitation of George V, Hind had the audacity to boast to the king that his, Hind's, collection was better than the king's.

Rumor also has it—again, unconfirmed—that a second copy of the one-cent magenta surfaced later, and that Hind bought it and then burned it so that his copy would continue to be unique.

Hind was neither a philatelic scholar nor a particularly meticulous collector. When Hind's collection came to market after his death, the philatelic world was horrified to discover that he had mounted stamps with adhesive tape, poor-quality glue, or anything else handy, without the slightest thought to the damage they would cause. As a result, many priceless rarities were permanently discolored or disfigured and, when auctioned, sold for far less they might otherwise have.

Unlike the Ferrari and Hind collections, George V's remained intact after his death, and today resides in Buckingham Palace, part of the Royal Philatelic Collection. Each successive monarch, including Queen Elizabeth II, has added to it.

Other prominent stamp collectors include William H. Crocker (1861–1937), a California banker and financier; Alfred Caspery (1868–1955), investment banker; Josiah K. Lilly, Jr. (1893–1966), the pharmaceutical magnate; Theodore Steinway (1883–1957) of piano manufacturing fame; King Farouk of Egypt (1920–1965); President Franklin

D. Roosevelt (1882-1945); and Colonel Edward H. R. Green (1868–1936), son of the fabulously wealthy Hetty Green, to name just a few.

Colonel Edward H. R. "Ned" Green is best remembered for having purchased the intact sheet of inverted Jennies in 1918. Green did not take up stamp collecting until midlife, when, so the story goes, he bought a packet of stamps for a friend's son in 1916 at the Scott Stamp and Coin Co. in New York and liked them so much he kept them. So smitten was he that he returned to Scott Stamp and Coin Co. the following day and bought $31,000 more.

Ned's mother, Hetty Green, the infamous "Witch of Wall Street," had amassed a fortune worth $100 million but was a miser of unrivaled proportion. She made a home for her two children, Ned and Sylvia, in a cold-water flat in Hoboken, New Jersey, that rented for less than $20 a month when she could easily have afforded better. At the time she owned several thousand real estate properties and had tens of millions outstanding in short-term loans and mortgages, all at high interest rates. Yet she dressed in cheap clothes, worked in an unheated office, warmed her lunch of oatmeal on the radiator of an office neighbor, and haggled over the price of everything, including groceries. When young Ned injured his leg in a sledding accident, Hetty dressed him in ill-fitting clothes and took him to the Bellevue Hospital Free Clinic for treatment. A few days later, when the staff learned of Hetty's identity, they demanded payment, which she refused. Instead, she bundled Ned up, took him home, and treated his leg with poultices and patent medicine. His leg was never right after that, and a few years later doctors had to amputate it above the knee. Green was forced to walk with a wooden leg for the rest of his life.

Upon Hetty's death in 1916, Ned and his sister, Sylvia, inherited the fortune. Ned set about spending his share with as much enthusiasm as his mother had displayed accumulating it. He built a million-dollar mansion, staffed it with more than a hundred employees, bought the biggest yacht in the world, built his own private airfield, and bought a radio station, which he ordered to play nothing but music he liked. Green stood six feet four inches and weighed more than 275 pounds. He was a large man with large appetites. Over the course of the next twenty years he ate, drank, caroused, and collected with gusto, amassing one of the largest hoards of stamps ever assembled.

The stamps, purchased both singly and in collections, ranged from the common to the rare and elusive. There seemed no rhyme or reason to his acquisitions. Unlike other great collectors who became philatelic scholars, connoisseurs or highly focused collection builders, Green remained the consummate acquisitor, buying whatever struck his fancy, then promptly forgetting he owned it. He lacked both discipline and focus, but never seemed to be aware of it. He loved errors above all other kinds of stamps, which led him to the purchase of the sheet of Jenny inverts, as well as more than a dozen of the rare 1869 inverts, dozens of the 1901 Pan American inverts, and 28 of the 49 known complete sheets of the imperforate 5-cent color error.

Green died in 1936. Eight years later, his massive hoard came to market. In terms of sheer bulk, it was the largest holding of stamps ever to come to market, amounting to more than 50,000 lots spread over 28 auctions held between 1942 and 1946. At the time Green's collection was broken up, it still contained 41 of Green's original purchase of 100 Jenny inverts. The series of 28 auction sales yielded more than $1,800,000, which should be multiplied by at least a factor of 10 to get an idea of value in current dollars.

King Farouk of Egypt was another large man with large appetites. Before being deposed in 1952, the arrogant and egotistical monarch enjoyed the singular advantage of not only being able to order his own likeness on postage stamps, but having the ability to create proofs, imperforates, and other rarities whenever the whim moved him, which was often. Farouk squandered money on a lavish lifestyle —parties, travel, automobiles, jewels, mistresses—at a time when most Egyptians scraped along at subsistence levels. After Egypt came out on the short end in the war with Israel in 1948, the military began to grumble, and in 1952, fed up with Farouk's extravagance and ineptitude, deposed him. The playboy king settled in Monaco,

King Farouk of Egypt.

where he continued his opulent lifestyle until an early death at age forty-five in 1965.

President Franklin D. Roosevelt is perhaps the best-known American stamp collector. He took up stamp collecting as a boy and continued throughout his life, taking an active role in the decision-making process of all stamps issued during his administration. Roosevelt appointed his campaign manager and long-time political adviser, James A. Farley, postmaster general. Together they had a ball with stamps, and so did the stamp collectors of America. Farley seemed to enjoy philately, or at least the publicity surrounding it, as much as FDR enjoyed collecting. Farley loved staging media events, making a big show of autographing the first sheet of stamps off the press for his friend President Roosevelt, basking in the glare of newsreel camera lights, energized by the staccato bursting of flashbulbs.

Franklin D. Roosevelt.

Farley gave press sheets to his friends as well. When one of Farley's friends tried to pledge his uncut, imperforate, ungummed press sheet as collateral for a loan of several thousand dollars—pointing out to the loan officer that imperforate sheets could not be obtained by the public and were therefore very valuable—collectors cried foul. FDR's political enemies jumped on the bandwagon. The public was outraged that the postmaster general appeared to be profiting from his position, to the tune of thousands of dollars, a fortune during the Depression. Most Americans earned less than $50 a month and considered themselves lucky just to have a job at the time. Congress finally forced Farley to make the ungummed, imperforate stamps available to the public. Ironically, in reissuing them, the post office reaped an enormous dividend. The demand for "Farley's Follies" translated into more than $1,500,000 in sales, most of it pure profit because few of the stamps ever saw postal duty.

No one ever suggested that President Roosevelt requested special stamps or special treatment. Evidence suggests that Farley, not a collector himself, actually distributed the press sheets as souvenirs, unaware that they would be worth a lot of money or that anyone would consider it improper.

FDR brought a keen sense of philatelic aesthetics and American history to the stamps issued during his presidency. He believed United States postage stamps should have dignity and merit. He vetoed subjects he felt were not worthy of the honor. The more than 200 stamps issued during his twelve-year presidency include some of the most beautiful, best-designed stamps ever issued by the United States, such as the National Parks set, Famous Americans set, and the Presidential series. They celebrate the unique egalitarian majesty of our culture and possess a quality of unassuming nobility that American stamps have not exhibited since.

CHAPTER 10

CONSERVATION

Stamps, especially old ones, are fragile objects that must be handled and stored with care. The three great enemies of stamps are light, heat, and moisture. Avoid these hazards as much as possible.

Don't display stamps in direct light for prolonged periods. Pigments are prone to fading, paper to yellowing. Sunlight is especially bad; fluorescent light not much better. Even the use of UV glass to screen out ultraviolet light will not protect against other wavelengths, which, can also cause damage over time, although more subtly. Short-term exposure to light, such as exhibiting at a show, is not a danger.

More stamps are ruined by moisture than by any other hazard. Moisture in all forms (water, humidity, dampness) is deadly. Keep stamps as dry as possible. Always store stamp albums upright so they can breathe. Never store albums flat, especially piled one atop another, because the weight causes stamps to stick, especially under humid conditions. Even stamps in glassines are susceptible to moisture and pressure. Once they are stuck together, only soaking will separate them, and their gum will be lost. Album paper absorbs humidity just like a sponge, but loses it only slowly. A few humid days can expose stamps to weeks of dampness. Open albums and allow them to dry any time they have been exposed to abnormal humidity. Humidity wreaks such havoc on gum that some collectors in places such as Hawaii and the Caribbean islands collect only used stamps.

Moisture also promotes the growth of mold and mildew, which discolors stamps and attacks gum. Even stamps without gum are susceptible to mildew and foxing.

Avoid storing stamps in places prone to dampness or leaks, such as basements, storage sheds, and barns. Don't store stamps near water pipes. Even safe-deposit boxes are not one hundred percent safe. In some cases, stamps in fireproof bank vaults have been ruined by sprinklers set off by a fire in another part of the bank (we have no idea what sprinklers were doing inside a *fireproof* vault). Occasionally, safe-deposit vaults located below ground level are flooded by broken water mains or springtime downpours, perils that do not affect vaults located above ground. Subterranean vaults are also more prone to dampness from ground water.

Keep stamps away from heat, which compounds the effects of moisture. Avoid storing stamp albums on shelves exposed to direct sunlight. Avoid attics and garages, which are likewise prone to overheating. Exposure to heat and moisture causes stamps to curl, often so badly that attempting to uncurl them ruins them. Dry heat is no better. It causes stamps to become brittle and gum to crack, which in severe cases breaks through a stamp's paper, ruining it. Prolonged exposure to dramatic temperature swings weakens a stamp's paper fibers over time, just as repeatedly bending a piece of wire weakens it.

Keep stamps away from dust and dirt. Wind-blown grit, the kind that accumulates in garages and sheds, acts like sandpaper, if ever so subtly. Keep stamps away from insects. Even seemingly innocuous ones can be dangerous. Crickets love the flavor of some gums and eagerly nibble away portions of stamps possessing it.

A few more don'ts. Never use any kind of tape to mount stamps or covers. Keep tape—adhesive, cellophane, whatever the kind—away from your collection. Don't use it on stamps, on album pages, on glassines, or to secure the sides of mounts. Don't use tape on anything stamp-related—period.

Don't mount or store newspaper clippings next to stamps. Newspaper yellows and degrades with the passing of time. The chemicals that cause yellowing migrate into any other papers they come in contact with—stamps, covers, album pages. Discard old glassines or anything else that has yellowed with age. The jury's still out on recycled paper, which is treated with chemicals to bleach and whiten it. In general, avoid papers with a strong chemical odor. It may take years to know what effects, if any, recycling chemicals have on paper. Meanwhile, avoid taking risks with your stamps.

Keep rubber bands away from stamps. They contain a sulfur compound that discolors some pigments. There's nothing worse than a rubber band that's dried out or melted and adhered to whatever it's come in contact with.

Don't use paper clips on stamps or anywhere that might leave a mark on stamp. Some paper clips rust, especially in humid climates, leaving spots on anything they've come in contact with.

Don't soak stamps on colored paper (such as those used to mail Christmas cards) with stamps on white paper. Colored papers, especially red, bleed badly when wet, discoloring any stamps soaked with them. Experienced collectors don't even bother soaking stamps on red paper.

Avoid storing stamps in anything made of softened plastic such as vinyl. The softer the plastic, the more softening agent it contains (visible as an oily, iridescent film). The softening agent, which is petrochemical-based, has been known to leech the color out of some printing inks and to discolor stamps. Unsoftened (free of softening agent) vinyl is fairly inert.

Don't store stamps in variety-store photo albums, especially the kind with waxed or self-adhesive pages, even those advertised as low-tack.

Never try to force a stamp into a mount too

small or too tightly fitting. Either you'll damage the stamp right then, or it will warp with the passing of time. Always use a mount large enough to accommodate a stamp comfortably. And be careful not to use too much saliva on the back of a mount. The excess will leak onto the back of the stamp, defeating the whole purpose of the mount.

Don't hinge never hinged stamps. You'll reduce their value. It's okay to hinge used stamps and stamps with no gum.

Don't remove stamps from covers or postcards; they usually have more value than the stamps by themselves. Don't attempt to separate stamps that are stuck together or stuck down to album pages; you'll only cause damage and reduce their value. Don't attempt to clean stamps; you'll do more harm than good.

A few do's:

Fingers contain moisture, oil, and often small amounts of grime. Make sure your hands are clean before working with stamps, and always use stamp tongs to handle stamps.

Use materials made specifically for the hobby. If a material wasn't made for stamps, think twice about using it.

Insure stamps if they have any significant value. Most homeowner's policies cover collectibles, but their limits of liability are low, typically $300 or so, without a special rider. The APS offers an excellent, low-cost policy that covers most risks, such as fire or theft. Its policy's limits of liability are higher and premiums lower than those of most standard casualty policies. Check the resource guide under Stamp Insurance for the APS's address. Insurance is often less expensive than paying safe-deposit rent, especially for bulky collections. Before spending hundreds of dollars a year on storage, compare the cost with insurance. Be aware that unless the contents of a safe-deposit box are insured, they're at risk from loss by fire, theft, natural disaster, etc. Almost all banks refuse to accept liability for the contents of a safe-deposit box for any reason. Check your box rental agreement.

In summary, use common sense in handling and storing stamps. Keep them away from light, heat, moisture, and dirt. Avoid storing stamps in basements, garages, storage sheds, and attics. To the degree possible, store stamps in an area with constant temperature and humidity. Use high-quality materials, those intended specifically for use with stamps, where possible. Insure stamps if they have any significant value.

$\mathscr{E}$RRORS ON STAMPS

Everyone who buys stamps is playing the post office lottery whether he or she knows it or not. If you're lucky enough to find a roll of stamps without perforations, don't take it back and complain, don't cut the stamps apart; instead, contact an error dealer. You, too, may have won the post office lottery.

Today, stamp production is nearly one hundred percent automated. The touch of a button starts a press the size of a freight car rolling, an enormous roll of paper begins turning, and stamps flow out the other end, printed, perforated, and packaged—never touched by human hand, never seen by human eye. When humans performed quality control inspections, few errors escaped their vigilance. Today, with billions of stamps being printed every year, it's simply not feasible for humans to perform inspections. Machines do it, almost as well as humans but not quite. Errors slip out—not many, just a few of the billions and billions of stamps printed every year. So few as to be statistically insignificant. So few as to make them rare and valuable.

Major errors are the most valuable. They can be worth more than $100,000 (in cases such as the inverted Jenny), although most are worth substantially less. A major error is defined as the complete omission of perforations, the complete omission of one or more colors on a multicolored stamp, the inversion of one of the printed elements of the design, or the printing of a stamp in the wrong color. All traces of perforations between stamps must be absent (including faint impressions that do not break the paper, known as blind perfs) in order for an item to be considered an imperforate error. The color(s) described as omitted must be *completely* omitted in order for an item to be considered a color-omitted error. Even a trace of color disqualifies it from being considered a major error.

The term "major error" is used to distinguish stamps with major omissions from those with minor production imperfections, which are known as EFOs (errors, freaks, and oddities). Multitudes of EFOs exist, and include items such as misperfs (perforations shifted into the design or away from it), foldovers (stamps containing paper inadvertently folded back on itself during printing), ink smears, over- or underinking, and color shifts (one or more colors out of register). EFOs are usually worth only a few dollars each. Stamps containing design errors (such as the wrong number of stars on a flag) are generally not considered errors in the philatelic sense (unless a corrected version is released and the term "error" is used to distinguish the two) and have no particular value above and beyond their ordinary value as stamps.

The most commonly encountered major error is the imperforate coil stamp. The value of imperforate coil stamps ranges from a few dollars per stamp to more than $1,000 per stamp, depending on the

Imperforate coil pair.

Emily Dickinson commemorative with color omitted (left); normal (right).

quantity discovered. Generally, imperforate sheet stamps are worth more than imperforate coil stamps because fewer are discovered. And of the sheet stamps, imperforate commemoratives are usually worth more than imperforate definitives, again because they tend to be rarer. Very few imperforate booklets slip out; they tend to be the rarest. All the preceding are generalizations, and exceptions exist. With regard to errors, the final arbiter of value is quantity.

Generally—but not always—stamps with a color or colors omitted are worth more than imperforates because they are discovered less frequently, they tend to surface in smaller quantities, and they tend to be more visually striking. And given comparable scarcity, the more visually striking a color-omitted error, the more valuable. Color-omitted errors can be very subtle, so check stamps carefully.

$1 Rush Lamp and Flame with flame inverted.

Collectors and dealers are generally suspicious of used stamps that purport to have colors omitted because used stamps are so susceptible to bleaching and chemical treatment.

Inverts are rare. Since the United States began printing stamps in 1847, only about a dozen inverts have been discovered. The most famous is the inverted Jenny. One of the more recent U.S. inverts, the $1 Rush Lamp and Flame with the flame inverted (discovered in 1986), has been selling in the $12,500-to-$15,000 price range, which makes the aggregate value of the discovery (95 stamps) more than $1 million.

The value of a newly discovered error is never clear, either to the dealer or to the finder, and ultimately depends on how many more like it surface—and how quickly. There is no absolute ratio of quantity to price, but generally a modern (post-1950) major error for which fewer than twenty-five examples are known sells for thousands of dollars; for which less than a couple of hundred are known sells for hundreds; and for which more than a thousand are known sells for less than $25. There are exceptions, but you can see how quickly price falls as quantity rises. Classic major errors sell for more than modern major errors of comparable quantity, by virtue of their age, their charisma, and long market history.

Finders of major errors face a dilemma: hold out for top dollar and hope no more surface, or take what the market offers and eliminate the risk. The value of an initial discovery diminishes in proportion to the magnitude of the additional discoveries. Dealers, too, face a dilemma: offer a high price to beat out competition and pray no more surface, or sit on the sidelines and wait for the market to sort itself out.

The answer is never clear and usually depends on buyers' and sellers' perception of the odds. A roll of 100 imperforate definitive flag stamps contains 50 pairs (imperforates are collected in pairs or multiples because singles can be created by trimming perforations off). Flag definitives usually have an extended life, often several years, during which time many billions are printed. Experience has shown that not only do definitive coils invariably show up imperforate, but that over time they show up in large numbers. The best bet—if you play the odds—with that type of error is to sell into the market right away.

Commemorative imperforates are much scarcer because they remain on sale for only a limited time. The same is true for commemorative color-omitted errors. The risk of additional quantities of a color-omitted commemorative surfacing is much less, but not zero.

In 1986, the initial discoverer of the AMERIPEX booklet—a commemorative booklet—with black omitted sold his find for $500 per booklet. Ten more booklets surfaced within a week and the buy price dropped to $250 per booklet. Immediately thereafter, 100 more turned up and the price plummeted to $75. Then 300 more surfaced, then 500 more, and the price sank to $35 per booklet, then $20, and finally $15. Shortly thereafter, thousands more surfaced, and sellers found them difficult to move at any price. The market for AMERIPEX black-omitted error booklets had fallen apart in less than ten days.

Conversely, when about 25 pairs of the nondenominated "C" coil stamp turned up imperforate in 1981, dealers were reluctant to offer much for it because odds favored more coming to market. The "C" coil was, after all, a definitive, albeit a nondenominated transitional one, and dealers knew that hundreds of millions had been printed. The discoverer estimated the pairs to be worth $750 to $1,000 each. Dealers declined to buy, confident that more would surface, possibly hundreds or even thousands of pairs. It could easily end up a $10 pair, they reasoned. So the owner kept the stamps. Time passed. No more imperforate "C" coil stamps turned up. It became one of the rarest modern imperforate coils and now sells for between $1,000 and $2,000 per pair. Newly discovered major errors present risks for buyer and seller alike. All you can do is play the odds.

TIP: Don't make too much noise if you find an error. Rumors fly in the stamp business. A chance remark about a new discovery passing enough pairs of lips leaves the impression that many more of the error exist than actually do. That impression can only have a negative impact on dealers' perception of value and the size of their offers. Be discreet in your inquiries. Initially, contact one or two dealers specializing in error stamps, and go from there. *Top Dollar Paid: The Complete Guide to Selling Your Stamps* contains a more complete discussion on strategies for selling newly discovered major errors.

If you're interested in error stamps, join the Errors, Freaks, Oddities Collectors Club (EFOCC). The cost is nominal, and the club journal alone is worth the price of membership. *U.S. Errors: Inverts, Imperforates, and Colors Omitted on U.S. Postage Stamps* lists and prices all known U.S. major errors, including quantities known for most. It will give you a good feel for the effect of quantity on price, as well as make you aware of what to watch for.

Over the decades, hundreds of new major errors have been discovered by keen-eyed individuals who knew what to look for. Next time you buy a roll of stamps or a booklet, consider for a moment that you have a lottery ticket in your hand. The odds of winning are slim, but if you do, the payoff can be great. And the best part is that if you lose, you can use the stamps on mail just as you intended, and it cost you nothing to play!

*F*AKES AND FORGERIES

The terms "counterfeit," "forgery," "fake," and "bogus" are applied to stamps that are not legitimate. Fakes are not much of a problem for the general or casual collector buying moderately priced stamps. Cheap stamps are seldom faked, and when they are, the work is often crude and easy to spot. Dangerous fakes are most often encountered where real money is involved, and there the buyer needs to beware. This overview will not enable you to detect every bogus item, but it will make you aware that they exist and that you need to be alert. Several excellent books on the subject exist and are mentioned in the text below.

FAKES

Dangerous fakes of some stamps exist. Faking is nothing new. Many fakes were created decades ago, so the fact that a stamp has been in a collection for fifty years has little bearing on its genuineness.

POSTAL COUNTERFEITS. Counterfeits manufactured to defraud the post office are rare. Apparently, those willing to risk jail for counterfeiting prefer printing currency. In fact, postal counterfeits are so rare that they're usually worth more than their genuine counterparts. The allies counterfeited German stamps during World War II for use on propaganda mail dropped inside the Third Reich. These, too, are prized by collectors and worth far more than their genuine counterparts.

PHILATELIC FORGERIES. These are known as forgeries rather than counterfeits because they are intended to defraud collectors rather than a postal service.

A number of master craftsmen (and more than a few talented amateurs) produced dangerous forgeries of classic foreign stamps during the nineteenth century and early twentieth century. They concentrated on rare, elusive, or expensive issues. Your risk of getting a classic forgery is small unless you're spending big bucks on individual stamps, in which case you should insist on an expert certificate with every stamp.

REPRODUCTIONS AND REPRINTS. You're much more likely to come across a reproduction or reprint than an out-and-out forgery. During the early days of the hobby, dealers routinely sold reprints and reproductions of rare stamps. They advertised them as reproductions; there was no intent to defraud. In fact, one dealer ad urged collectors not to waste money on expensive originals when they could fill album spaces with excellent reproductions at little cost. Initially, no one thought there was anything wrong with making and selling reproductions and reprints. As the hobby grew more sophisticated, the philatelic community began to frown on the practice, and it stopped. Reprints and reproductions still turn up in old-time albums. They're known as album weeds because of the frequency with which they show. So, before you celebrate finding $10,000 worth of rare stamps, make sure they're not reproductions. Catalogues warn about which issues to watch out for and provide tips on how to identify many bogus stamps.

The fake coil at right was trimmed from a sheet stamp similar to that at left.

FAKE COILS. Coils are among the most frequently faked U.S. stamps. Expensive coil stamps are faked by trimming the perforations off parallel sides of an inexpensive sheet stamp of the same design. Fakes are usually narrower than genuine coils; the trimmed sides are often not parallel; and traces of perforations often remain visible on carelessly trimmed sides. The 1902–1903 definitive coils are frequently faked and should never be purchased without an expert certificate. Fake Washington-Franklin series coils are endemic. *The Expert's Book* by Paul Schmid is the best book on the subject of Washington-Franklin fakes and how to spot them. Later coils are seldom faked because they're neither rare nor expensive.

Line pairs (lines appear on rotary press coils where the printing plates were joined, about every 24 stamps or so) are sometimes faked by adding a line with a pen and ruler. Faked line pairs are seldom encountered and then only on expensive issues. Fake lines are easy to spot. A genuine line rises above the surface of the stamp's paper, because the nature of the intaglio printing process. You can feel it with your finger. Lines added by pen are perfectly smooth.

Expensive booklet panes are sometimes created by trimming the perforations from less expensive sheet stamps. Make sure booklet panes have large margins on the straightedged sides. Trimming off perforations leaves abnormally small margins, a sure sign of tampering.

FAKE CANCELS. In some cases, catalogue values for used copies of scarce stamps are the same as or more than for mint copies. A heavily hinged mint stamp, worth only a small fraction of catalogue, can be transformed into a very fine used copy, worth a greater percentage of catalogue, by soaking off the disturbed gum and applying a light cancel.

Generally, the greater the disparity in price between used and mint—when a used stamp catalogues more than a mint stamp—the more suspicious you should be.

Fake cancels and ancillary markings are sometimes added to increase the value of a cover. Stamps are sometimes added to stampless covers and tied with fake cancels, or low-denomination stamps lifted off and replaced with high denominations,

This German stamp is worth less than $20 mint, but $3,000 to $4,000 with genuine cancel.

which are rare on cover and worth much more on cover than off cover. Nineteenth-century covers are the usual targets for this type of trickery, and specialists are most often at risk because they are the primary market for rare covers.

Check cancels carefully on expensive covers. Many fakes are surprisingly obvious if you just pay attention. Be aware that fakes exist; don't begin to worry that every item is a fake.

FAKE ERRORS. Imperforate singles are faked by trimming the perforations off perforated copies, especially those with jumbo margins. That's why no one collects imperforate singles.

Fake used color-omitted errors are most often created by bleaching or exposing stamps to chemical treatment. Collectors generally ignore even genuine used color-omitted errors. They sell for little. Only a few mint color-omitted errors have ever been faked because exposure to chemical agents affects gum and makes tampering easy to spot. The Copernicus commemorative of 1973 with yellow omitted is one of the few mint errors that has been successfully faked. An expert certificate is essential when buying this stamp. Stamps whose color has been altered (as opposed to removed) by chemical treatment are known as changelings, and have no philatelic value whatsoever.

Catalogues generally warn about issues susceptible to faking, so check carefully before buying.

OVERPRINTS AND SURCHARGES. Overprints and surcharges are sometimes faked to turn inexpensive stamps into expensive varieties. Cheap stamps with overprints are seldom faked.

In the late 1920s, rural post offices in Kansas and Nebraska suffered a rash of burglaries. To make it more difficult to sell stamps stolen in those states elsewhere, the postal service overprinted then current definitives with either "Kans." or "Nebr." The experiment didn't have much impact on the thefts, and the postal service abandoned it after a short time. Kansas-Nebraska overprints were scarce from the beginning, and fakes started turning up right away.

Fake Kansas-Nebraska overprints most often appear on used stamps because the raw material (unoverprinted definitives) is abundant and cheap. Most Kansas-Nebraska fakes are laughably amateurish and easy to spot. Genuine overprints were applied by printing press. Fakes are frequently rubber-stamped or typewritten. Stamp pad ink is grayer than the solid black printer's ink, and the hole left by a typed period is a dead giveaway. Fakers also make the mistake of overprinting the wrong perforation variety. Genuine Kansas-Nebraska overprints always gauge perf $10\frac{1}{2}\times11$, not perf 10 or perf 11.

The easiest way to spot

Stamp of the Kansas-Nebraska issue with genuine overprint.

fakes of any kind is by comparison with known genuine examples. Fakers can never precisely match the subtleties of an original. Pay attention to catalogue footnotes that warn of fake overprints.

IMPROVEMENTS

It may be perfectly respectable, even desirable, to restore fine art or vintage automobiles, but not stamps. Improvements, or any other alteration, are the kiss of death in philately. The premiums commanded by high-quality stamps opened the door to "improvements."

REGUMMING. A regummed stamp has had new gum applied to simulate its original gum. Regumming is a fact of life. Buyers should be aware of the risk, but not intimidated by it. The attempt is often clumsy and amateurish, easy to spot with a little practice. However, clever and dangerous regumming jobs exist, especially coming out of Europe, where gum is applied by airbrush and other sophisticated techniques. Skilled regumming jobs are difficult to detect except by professionals who handle stamps every day, but most are easy to spot if you know what to look for. Compare the gum on a suspect stamp with gum on other stamps of the same series, especially one- or two-cent denominations, which are rarely regummed. If the gum looks markedly different, beware. Unevenly applied gum, thinly applied gum, gum speckled with dust or tiny air bubbles are all indications of regumming.

All mint nineteenth-century stamps should be examined for regumming, *especially* if offered as *never hinged*. The vast majority of so-called *never hinged* nineteenth-century U.S. stamps have been regummed. Be extremely cautious of expensive stamps, especially high values of the Columbian and Trans-Mississippi series. Some regummed stamps have even been lightly hinged to throw buyers off. Regumming is seldom encountered on stamps issued after 1920.

The best protection is to buy from a reliable source, especially if you're buying expensive stamps. Regumming is a problem only if you're not aware of it. Learn to spot signs of tampering. Insist on expert certificates with expensive stamps. And don't be afraid to ask dealers what to look for. They're usually happy to show you, and one look is worth a thousand words.

REPERFORATING. A reperforated stamp has had perforations added to simulate original perforations. This is done either to improve centering (infrequently) or get rid of a straightedge (frequently). Collectors disdain straight-edged stamps so much that they typically sell for only 10 or 20 percent of catalogue. Reperforating is most often encountered on stamps that were issued in panes with straight edges on one or two sides, such as the Columbian Exposition issue of 1893 and the Trans-Mississippi issue of 1898. Stamps issued in panes without straightedges are rarely reperforated.

Again, half the battle is just being aware of the problem. A stamp's perforation consists of two elements: the size of the hole and the spacing between the holes. Reperforators often get the spacing between holes right, but not the size of the hole. Experienced collectors test a suspect stamp by laying it atop a known genuine example (an inexpensive one- or two-cent value from the same set works well, too). Compare the perforations. If they don't match, the stamp's likely been reperforated. Be suspicious of any stamp with a row of flat perforation tops. Normal teeth are somewhat roughened when stamps are pulled apart, not left flat is if cut by scissors. Again, ask a dealer to demonstrate techniques for spotting straight-edges, and get a copy of *How to Detect Damaged, Altered, and Repaired Stamps,* by Paul Schmid. It's one of the best books on "improvements." Profusely illustrated, it covers regumming, reperforating, and other alterations in detail. Every serious collector should own a copy.

OTHER IMPROVEMENTS. Be alert for thins. When held up to the light, thin spots appear lighter than surrounding paper. When dipped in watermark fluid, thin spots appear darker than surrounding paper. Watch out for filled thins, i.e., thins that have been touched up with a paste of paper fibers, often applied with an artist's brush. Filled thins usually show up a different shade of white when dipped in watermark fluid. Some stamps have been regummed over filled thins. They, too, show up in watermark fluid.

Watch for ironed-out creases. Although often invisible to the naked eye, they're easy to spot in watermark fluid, showing up as dark lines. Pay attention to corner creases, which are often so slight as not to be noticed unless one is looking for them.

Be on the lookout for retouched scuffs and scrapes on the fronts of stamps. They're often hidden by the careful application of colored ink to the affected areas. They are easy to spot if you take the time to look.

Small tears are often repaired with delicate adhesive such as egg white. You can usually spot these with the naked eye or in watermark fluid.

In philately, the term "cleaned" refers to a stamp that's had its cancellation removed. Early nineteenth-century stamps are the ones most often cleaned. Stamps are cleaned to increase their value, either by making them appear unused or, in the case of pen-canceled stamps, by recanceling them with device cancels (grids, circular date stamps, etc.), which are worth more than pen cancels. Fakers prefer pen-canceled stamps for cleaning because writing ink is more susceptible to bleaching than stamp pad ink, and because pen-canceled stamps are inexpensive compared to device-canceled stamps. Sometimes bleached-out cancels show up in watermark fluid; however, ultraviolet light works better and in almost all cases reveals the tampering.

Improvements and faults are so often encountered on nineteenth-century stamps that it's second nature for experienced collectors and dealers to hold them up to the light or dip them in watermark fluid to check for problems.

Expert Certificates

Expert certificates are advisable for stamps prone to fakery and for expensive stamps. Stamps are expertized for authenticity, for gum and perforations, for use on cover, and for faults. You can request that a purchase be subject to confirmation by expert opinion. If the seller refuses, think twice. Sellers should be aware that dealers usually pay more for expensive stamps with expert certificates. *The Buyer's Guide: An Analysis of Selected U.S. Postage Stamps* advises—on a stamp-by-stamp basis—when expertizing is necessary.

The Philatelic Foundation and the American Philatelic Expertizing Service are the two foremost expertizing bodies in the United States. Neither deals in stamps; they are impartial and their opinions highly respected throughout the philatelic community. Write for a submission form and fee schedule *before* sending a stamp to either service for an opinion. Both bodies issue certificates containing a color photograph of the subject stamp together with a summary of their findings. Fees are based on the value of the stamp (or cover), with a minimum fee applicable for items of nominal value or for items that turn out not to be genuine. Turn-around time is

American Philatelic Expertizing Service expert certificate.

typically four to eight weeks. Consult the resource guide for their addresses.

Any discussion of fakes makes the problem sound worse than it is. Fakes most often afflict expensive stamps, and most fakes can be spotted if you are reasonably attentive. Be alert, pay attention to catalogue cautions, be diligent in examining nineteenth-century stamps and those prone to fakery, and know when to expertize.

THE MARKET IN A NUTSHELL

The stamp market is more than 150 years old. It is broad and deeply rooted, with dealers spread across the world in most major cities and many small towns as well. They range in size from small mom-and-pop operations to public corporations with multimillion-dollar budgets, and they buy and sell stamps every day. As a result, stamps are highly liquid. American dealers are as close as the Yellow Pages, or if you live off the beaten path, the American Stamp Dealers Association (ASDA) maintains a no-cost referral service that will provide the addresses and telephone numbers of the dealers near you upon receipt of a business-size, self-addressed, stamped envelope.

The stamp market is subject to all the economic factors that influence other markets: optimism and pessimism; inflation and deflation; boom and recession; interest rates, currency fluctuations, and speculation. Sometimes prices are strong, other times not. Over the long term, however, stamp prices (for high-quality material) rise and generally keep pace with inflation or beat it. Stamp values have increased about 500 percent in the last fifty years, or about ten percent per year without compounding.

The market for any nation's stamps is based in the country of its origin. Developed nations with thriving economies have large, affluent collector bases; undeveloped nations and tiny island nations do not.

There is always a market for scarce, high-quality stamps of the United States, western Europe, the British Commonwealth, and the Far East.

Mint never hinged sets and singles of the world issued during the period 1930–1970 always seem to be in demand. Demand for hinged copies of the period is not as great. Most used stamps of the period are abundant.

Except for topical sets and singles, demand is limited for stamps of Central and South America and for Africa. The same can be said for the small island nations of the Caribbean and the Pacific, which export nearly 100 percent of the stamps they print.

Demand is strong for scarce, quality mint sets from Western Europe and the Far East, especially those of Germany, Japan, and China. During the desperate years immediately following World War II, collectors in former Axis countries could not afford to buy mint stamps, and collectors in other countries had little interest in stamps of their former enemies. Now an affluent generation of German and Japanese collectors needs them, and prices for German and Japanese mint stamps of the postwar decade have risen sharply, and likely will continue to do so. Some (especially commemoratives and semipostals) are scarce used, too, but demand is not as great for them as for mint stamps.

Chinese stamps experienced a different problem during the Cultural Revolution of the late 1960s, but with a similar result. Party zealots condemned stamp collecting as a petty-bourgeois pastime. At the same time, the party churned out a steady stream of stamps praising Chairman Mao and the Cultural Revolution, but few were saved. Now that the Chinese are less dogmatic and more affluent, demand for Chinese stamps of all eras is growing rapidly.

Stamps of Vietnam are in demand both in the United States and abroad, as is postal history of the Vietnam War.

Stamps of Eastern Europe are in demand, too, now that the Soviet Union has disintegrated. Russian collectors are increasingly affluent and no longer fear owning czarist stamps.

The stamp market is simply too broad to cover adequately here; besides, it fluctuates. The best way to keep up with what's going on is to read philatelic periodicals, and network with fellow collectors and stamp dealers. Remarks such as "Japan's hot" or "Vatican's cooled way off" (hypothetical remarks, by the way) tell the story. News about market trends spreads quickly.

Any discussion of the market inevitably raises the question of investment. Stamps do not possess some special, magical attribute for profit. As with any commodity, some stamps are good investments; many others are not. If you're buying stamps purely for investment, your success will be directly proportional to the amount of knowledge, homework, and experience you bring to the task.

That said, one of the advantages of philately is that when you've finished enjoying your collection, the stamps have residual value. That value should be regarded as a bonus, not the *raison d'être* for collecting. Ironically, it is often those collections built up over a lifetime by dedicated collectors with no thought whatsoever of profit that prove to be the most profitable. Collections carefully assembled by knowledgeable collectors contain the type of material in demand by other advanced collectors—buyers with both the motivation and the money.

If you're buying for appreciation, concentrate on rarity and quality. There's always a demand for carefully formed collections of any nation or specialty containing balanced runs of premium stamps.

Those who have inherited or acquired a collection but have no real interest in stamps often ask, "Should I hold on to it? Will it appreciate in value?

Or should I sell it?" Compare the anticipated future value of the collection with that of an alternate investment. Go with the higher yield.

If the collection consists of common, low-priced stamps, you'll likely be ahead selling the stamps and investing the proceeds elsewhere. Time alone works no magic on the value of common stamps. If the collection consists of scarce, high-quality stamps, then consider keeping it. Before making a decision, find out how the stamps in the collection have performed over the last decade or so. If you decide to keep it, remember that stamps do best over the long term. They are generally not good short-term investments. If you're not familiar with stamps, you should consider holding them as an investment only if you enjoy them. If you're not interested in stamps, convert them to cash and put the money into something you understand. You will probably have better luck.

In summary, the stamp market is broad and well established. The market for any nation's stamps is rooted in its domestic market. Affluent, developed countries generally have the strongest stamp markets. Weigh any decision to hold stamps purely for investment against potential returns elsewhere. Concentrate on scarce, high-quality stamps. Cheap stamps rarely appreciate significantly. Hold stamps for investment only if you enjoy them. Be prepared to hold them for the long term.

$\mathcal{D}$ISPOSING
OF A COLLECTION

Stamp dealers can't restock by calling a factory; they must rely on stamps obtained from collectors, other dealers, or auctions to replenish their stocks. They're keenly aware that they are in competition with one another, and that an offer is likely to be measured against that of a competitor. That awareness motivates them to make competitive offers and guarantees the seller a good price.

APPRAISAL AND OFFER

The terms "appraisal "and "offer" are often confused. An appraisal is a valuation by an expert and not necessarily an offer to buy. Stamps are appraised for many purposes: insurance (usually replacement cost), estates (usually market value), legal settlements, divorces, judgments, etc.—and, of course, for outright sale. Replacement value is the retail cost of replacing stamps; market value is the amount one would expect to receive selling to a dealer. In most cases, an appraisal is a formal, written evaluation for which the owner pays a fee.

If you're unfamiliar with stamps or the stamp market, it's helpful to have an appraisal made before soliciting offers, especially if your collection is large or potentially valuable. Dealers charge either by the hour, typically $25 to

$50 per hour (more if the dealer travels to your location), or a percentage of the value, typically starting at 2½ percent and dropping as the dollar value of the collection increases. Fees are negotiable on large-dollar properties. A minimum fee usually applies, regardless of the collection's value. Most dealers refund their appraisal fee if they end up buying the collection.

Always have an appraisal done by a professional; don't rely on an amateur or a fellow collector. It's not that a fellow collector's not honest or trustworthy; he simply won't have the intimate knowledge of the stamp market and up-to-the-minute values that a professional has. And don't rely on dealers in other fields, such as antiques or autographs, for a reliable evaluation. They may be knowledgeable in their own fields, but no one is as knowledgeable about stamps and the stamp market as a stamp dealer.

An offer is a dealer's spot cash price. There is usually no charge for making an offer, but some dealers refuse to make offers for free. Dealers who are reluctant to make an offer at no charge will often do so for a fee. They usually waive the fee or refund it if they subsequently buy the collection. In effect, they're giving an appraisal backed by cash. Getting two or three offers is usually sufficient to establish the value of a property. It's wise to have an idea of the value of your stamps so you can negotiate intelligently.

TELEPHONE EVALUATIONS

Don't expect an offer from a telephone description. The dealer *must* see the actual stamps in order to make an offer. Remember how small differences, such as perforation gauge and watermark, can mean the difference between a few cents and thousands of dollars? And how greatly prices vary with condition? And how faults and improvements affect value? The only way a dealer can accurately assess condition and grade is to see a stamp.

APS logo at left; ASDA logo at right.

SELECTING A DEALER

Select a reliable dealer. It's your best insurance for getting a good price. Don't hesitate to ask for references, the length of time a dealer has been in business (which should be a minimum of several years), or professional credentials, such as ASDA or APS dealer membership. Both groups screen dealer applicants and check references before admitting anyone to membership. Both the ASDA and the APS publish dealer directories. The APS directory is available at no cost to members. The ASDA directory is available for a fee. It lists member dealers, length of time in business, and specialty, together with addresses and telephone numbers. Refer to the resource directory. In addition, there are many completely reliable dealers across America who are not ASDA members.

Sell to the best market to obtain the best price. Most dealers are in the market for general U.S. or foreign collections and pay good prices for them. If your collection is large, specialized, or particularly valuable, you will often get the best price from a specialist. The APS and ASDA directories cross-reference dealers by specialty.

OUTRIGHT SALE

Outright sale is the most direct and simple way to dispose of stamps. Once a price is agreed upon, settlement is immediate; you walk away with cash in hand.

Auction

Sale by auction is also popular, especially for rare or valuable stamps. However, nothing—not even an auction—can work miracles on low-grade material. Outright sale is usually best for modest collections. The selling commission at auction is usually 10 percent of the hammer price, but can vary up or down depending on the size of the consignment. Each auction house has its own fee schedule. Auctions typically charge buyers a fee of either 10 percent or 15 percent also. Major auction houses usually require a minimum consignment of at least $1,000 net value; low profit margins make it uneconomical to handle smaller consignments. Many auctions offer advances, typically 50 percent of anticipated proceeds. Some auctions charge interest on advances, others do not. Auctions usually settle with consignors forty-five to sixty days after a sale. This allows time to collect payment from mail bidders.

Auction firms vary in size from small local houses to large national and international firms that routinely gross $500,000 to $3 million per sale. Some auctions are general; others specialize in U.S. stamps, foreign stamps, rarities, large lots, etc.

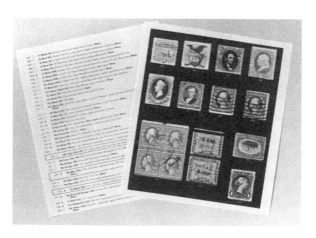

Pages from typical stamp auction catalogue.

Again, you will likely get a better price for a specialized collection selling through an auction catering to that specialty.

Stamp auctions are not like local estate, furniture, or barn sales. Each item (single stamp, set, or grouping) is examined, lotted separately, and described in detail. Lots are published in illustrated auction catalogues, which are mailed to thousands of collectors well in advance of the sale. Buyers bid either in person, by mail, or through agent. Before doing business with an auction, request a sample of one of its recent catalogues to get an idea of the size and quality of its operation. Generally, the larger a firm's mailing list, the better the results you'll get. The largest U.S. auction houses are on the East and West coasts and in big cities. They advertise regularly in philatelic periodicals.

Make sure that you understand all the elements of a consignment agreement before signing it. Most auctions have a minimum fee, for example, $100 (10 percent of the minimum net consignment of $1,000). If your consignment realizes only $800, you're still be liable for the minimum $100 commission. Most U.S. auctions do not charge lotting fees or illustration fees in addition to their basic commission. Look elsewhere if asked to pay lotting or illustration fees. Some auctions allow reserves. Expect to pay a commission (sometimes just the seller's portion, other times both buyer's and seller's portions) on reserved lots if they remain unsold. A better strategy is to ask the auctioneer to estimate how much your stamps will yield before consigning. If you don't like what you hear, don't waste your time consigning and reserving. Auctioneers sell stamps year in and year out; their estimates are usually within 10 percent of actual realizations.

TIP: the best time to auction stamps is during the cold-weather months—October through May. Summer months are notoriously slow in the stamp trade.

The advantage of selling by auction is the small cost of selling. The disadvantage is time. It usually takes six months from time of consignment to settlement. This can be partially offset by obtaining an advance.

PRIVATE TREATY

In a private treaty arrangement, the stamp dealer acts in the capacity of agent, receiving a commission for his services. Commissions vary depending upon the size and type of collection. The more sizable the property, the more negotiable the commission. Typical commissions range from 10 to 20 percent.

CONSIGNMENT FOR RETAIL SALE

Some dealers take stamps on consignment, typically paying for them as they sell. If you consign, get an agreement in writing, along with photocopies of your stamps, to avoid the possibility of confusion or disagreement later. The agreement should set forth the minimum price for each item, rate of commission, and terms for payout. There is no standard commission rate (commissions range from 10 percent to 40 percent), so expect to negotiate. Make sure the dealer has insurance and that it covers your stamps. The insured value of your consignment should be stated on the consignment agreement. Listen to the dealer's advice about pricing. Stamps priced unrealistically high only sit around and waste your time and the dealer's time.

Before entering into any consignment agreement check a dealer's credentials. Be suspicious of anyone who claims he can get unrealistically high prices. Such an approach is often the sign of an undercapitalized operation desperate for inventory, and when a shoestring operation goes out of business, the consignor is left holding the bag.

The disadvantages of consignment are that money comes in slowly over a period of time (typically many months) and only the better items tend to sell. Consignment is not recommended for the novice.

STAMP SHOWS

The concentration of dealers in one location at a stamp show offers an excellent opportunity to ask questions and shop for offers. You'll quickly learn the market value of your stamps and, if you wish, make a deal right on the spot.

Shows feature a cross section of dealers: local and out of town, large and small, general dealers and specialists. Rosters are available from show sponsors weeks before the show. Don't expect dealers to give you their full attention during prime time (late Friday and all day Saturday). They're usually busy with retail customers and do not want to be distracted. The best times to meet with show dealers are early Friday and Sunday mornings.

If your collection is too large to bring to the show, contact a dealer about coming to your home to view it while he's in town for a show. However, don't wait until the weekend of the show to try to make an appointment; the dealer may be booked up by then. Call well in advance. Information on upcoming stamp shows in your area is available in philatelic periodicals or by inquiring at a local dealer.

RETAILING YOUR STAMPS

Retailing your own stamps is a thankless task. In order to sell directly to the public, you must advertise, visit stamp clubs, take booths at stamp shows, or adopt some other retail strategy.

The advantages of retail sale are that you set the asking prices and you retain all profits.

The drawbacks are numerous. It takes a lot of time to prepare and make sales. Buyers tend to be picky. They buy only what they need to fill spaces. It usually takes months to liquidate an entire collection. Advertising is costly. Advertising in the local newspaper doesn't pull the kind of clientele you need. You get lots of lookers and bargain hunters, and sometimes unsavory characters casing your home, but few buyers.

Advertising in philatelic publications usually generates multiple orders for the choicest items, while the majority go begging. If you inadvertently price your material too high, you'll get no response. And the best buyers are reluctant to deal with new and unfamiliar names. You'll be amazed at the number of fussy buyers who disagree with your descriptions or grading and demand refunds. You'll also have to return checks or make refunds for items sold out. In short, mail order stamp dealing involves a great deal of correspondence.

Experience teaches that gross margin (markup) is not all profit, that many costs are involved, not the least of which is time. Stamp dealing, like any business, requires knowledge, time, trouble, and capital outlay. Most individuals who try retailing their stamps eventually throw up their hands in despair.

GIFTS

Making a gift is especially appropriate if your stamps have little market value but lots of eye appeal. Old albums and cigar-box accumulations delight youngsters, who treasure them far out of proportion to their real value.

HOW DEALERS VALUE COLLECTIONS

Stamps of all countries fall into two categories: key stamps and common stamps. Dealers check for keys, assess their individual condition, and calculate their value. Then they calculate the value of the balance. The majority of stamps of most countries were issued after World War II, and of these, the majority have low catalogue values, which tend to be fairly constant from stamp to stamp. The calculation of balances is really an exercise in bulk, e.g., 500 stamps at 20 cents each (or whatever value is appropriate) equals $100, and so forth. Each dealer has his own formula, but all formulas are based on the same principle: value the keys individually; value the balance in bulk. Nine out of ten collections, regardless of the country, lack most keys and consist largely of common stamps. Dealers see the same balances of common stamps year in and year out; they know their values well and tend to value them quickly. It is not uncommon for two different dealers to page quickly through the same multivolume collection and come up with figures less than 5 percent apart, even on collections worth $10,000 or $20,000.

Experienced stamp dealers acquire detective skills that enable them to quickly form opinions about collections from clues in both the stamps and the owners. Collectors are creatures of habit. Each has very specific acquiring and spending habits. A collector may not even be aware of his pattern, but it's readily apparent to the dealer. The keys in any given collection tend to hover near a certain maximum figure, be it $5, $50, or whatever. Further, it is quickly apparent whether an individual was condition-conscious or tolerated damaged stamps. Once the general nature of a collection reveals itself, the pattern rarely digresses. An experienced dealer knows right away what to expect in terms of value. One more point about value. Used albums and supplies, as well as the labor invested in mounting a collection, have no resale value.

WHAT TO LOOK FOR

Dealers zero in on quality and value. Here's what they look for and what you should look for.

Dealers look for complete sets and series, solid runs of better stamps. Short sets and spottiness are a sure sign of a mediocre collection, one without much value. And don't expect age to magically transform a thirty-year-old beginner album, on which a few dollars were spent, into a valuable property. Don't expect a collection formed from packets obtained at the five-and-dime to be suddenly worth hundreds or thousands of dollars. Valuable collections are formed over decades by methodical individuals who spend meaningful sums of money on better- than-average stamps.

Dealers look for mint stamps, and the more the better, especially twentieth-century stamps.

They look for high values (mint or used), the top denominations in sets and series. These are the keys to value. Low values are almost always cheap stamps, regardless of age. Remember that before the advent of telephones and electronic communication, everyone wrote letters, and they typically used the one-, two-, and three-cent denominations to mail them. These stamps are still common today. Exception: always check covers out carefully. They can be valuable for a variety of reasons not immediately apparent: postmarks, transit marks, and usage (such as pony express).

Dealers look for high-quality condition, especially on key stamps. Serious collectors don't tolerate damaged stamps in their collections. Ragtag pages, torn and taped, are not the mark of a sophisticated, knowledgeable collector. And unsophisticated collectors don't spend much on stamps.

Dealers look for quality albums and well-organized presentations. The fact that someone cared enough to buy an expensive album indicates that he probably bought quality stamps, too.

Dealers look for quantity: multivolume collections, boxes and glassines loaded with stamps, stock books stuffed with duplicates, and cartons bulging with covers. Sometimes what a collection lacks in quality, it makes up for in quantity. Nothing sets a dealer's mouth to watering like a large hoard.

DISCOUNTS FROM CATALOGUE

Sellers often ask dealers, "What discount from catalogue do you pay?" The answer is, there is no standard discount; it varies from item to item and from country to country. It varies between classic and modern, between mint and used, and between grades of condition. Some stamps are worth full catalogue, others are worth only a small fraction of catalogue. As we've mentioned, faulty nineteenth-century European used stamps are worth very little;

dealers pay 5 to 10 percent of catalogue for these. Demand for off-quality material is so low that dealers are reluctant to buy collections whose primary value arises from defective early stamps. Only nineteenth-century stamps in sound, VF or better, condition are worth a significant percentage of catalogue value.

As a rule, the greater the value of the stamp, the greater the percentage of catalogue you will get for it. The markup on a $2,000 stamp may be as little as $100 to $300. Markup on common stamps, packet material, kiloware, approvals, CTOs, etc., typically runs 100 to 500 percent, most of which goes toward handling and overhead.

As mentioned in the chapter on "The Market in a Nutshell," stamps of developed nations with large, established collector bases and robust domestic stamp markets tend to be worth more (in terms of percentage of catalogue value) than stamps from Third World countries. Third World nations to have very thin stamp markets and tend to rely on the topical appeal of their stamps for sales abroad.

Topical stamps for transient themes, such as World Refugee Year, are typically worth only a fraction of their new-issue price once the event has faded from prominence. Ongoing topicals, such as the Olympics, space, or flowers, hold their value better.

Modern U.S. first day covers (FDCs) and mass-marketed special-event covers are extremely abundant and, with few exceptions, worth only a fraction of their original price in the secondary market. By contrast, hand-painted FDCs and pre-1935 FDCs, both of which are scarce, tend to hold their value well.

Most mint U.S. stamps issued after 1945 trade at a discount from face value when sold in bulk to dealers; however, a number of stamps issued after 1981 are worth a premium. Check dealer buy ads in philatelic periodicals for exact quotes. Dealers pay less than face value for most post-1945 commemoratives because vast quantities were hoarded and still come on the market with great regularity—far more than can be absorbed by the collecting public. Most discount postage ends up used on mail. Dealers usually pay 80 percent and sell to bulk mailers at 90 percent. Each makes 10 percent for his trouble. Without the 10 percent incentive, neither would have any reason to buy and use large quantities of old postage. The exact discount depends on the market at the time of sale. Full sheets usually bring more than singles, blocks, or scrap, because they are easier to handle and count.

Why are 3-cent commemoratives that catalogue 15 cents worth only 80 percent of face value? The best analogy is "parts and labor": 3 cents parts and 12 cents labor. Even on those rare occasions when a 3-cent stamp sells for full catalogue, there is very little real profit for the dealer; the exercise is simply too time- and labor-intensive.

In summary, each stamp is valued according to its merits, and, generally, the more expensive the stamp, the greater its value in terms of percentge of catalogue value. There are so many variables involved in pricing that catalogues serve only as general guides, not absolutes.

GETTING A HANDLE ON PRICES

Check philatelic periodicals for retail advertisements and wanted-to-buy ads. They often quote prices for specific items, both U.S. and foreign. Compare buy prices and sell prices so that you learn to assess an offer and to negotiate intelligently. Talk to other collectors, note retail prices at shows, ask questions, and comparison-shop for offers.

The book *Top Dollar Paid: The Complete Guide to Selling Your Stamps* contains more detail about all aspects of selling, including negotiating, selling by mail, and when a dealer will travel to see a collection. Refer to the bibliography.

CHAPTER 15

INSTANT EXPERT QUIZ

1. Who invented the postage stamp?

2. What two elements determine a stamp's value?

3. What are the three greatest hazards to stamps?

4. What are the three most important elements of condition for a mint stamp?

5. What stamp is often referred to as the world's rarest stamp?

6. Name at least three essential philatelic tools.

7. What are the two essential functions of a stamp catalogue?

8. Name any two of the four types of major error stamps.

9. Name three ways of disposing of a stamp collection.

10. What is the difference between a counterfeit and a forgery?

11. What is the largest philatelic society in America?

12. What collector assembled the most comprehensive stamp collection in history?

13. On which nation's stamps does its name never appear?

14. Name a term used to describe larger than normal stamp margins.

15. What name is given to the type of collecting that focuses on things such as dogs, music, ships, or medicine?

16. What do the initials EKU stand for?

17. What is the difference between market value and replacement value?

18. In what year was the first stamp issued?

19. Who was America's best-known stamp collector?

20. What is a special occasion stamp?

Answers
1. *Sir Rowland Hill.*
2. *Rarity and quality.*
3. *Heat, light, and moisture.*
4. *Gum, hinging, and centering.*
5. *The British Guiana one-cent magenta of 1856.*
6. *Tongs, perforation gauge, watermark detector, catalogue, album, mounts, magnifying glass.*
7. *Identification and pricing.*
8. *Imperforate stamps, color-omitted stamps, inverts, stamps printed in the wrong color.*
9. *Outright sale, auction, private treaty, consignment, retailing on your own, and gift.*
10. *Counterfeits are created to defraud the postal service; forgeries are recreated to defraud collectors.*
11. *The American Philatelic Society (APS).*
12. *Count Philippe von Ferrari.*
13. *Great Britain.*
14. *Jumbo margins or boardwalk margins.*
15. *Topical collecting.*
16. *Earliest known use.*
17. *Market value is the amount one gets selling to a dealer; replacement value is full retail value.*
18. *1840.*
19. *Franklin D. Roosevelt.*
20. *Stamps such as Christmas or Love stamps.*

RESOURCE GUIDE

CHAPTER 16

DEALER ORGANIZATIONS

American Stamp Dealers Association (ASDA)
3 School Street, Suite 205
Glen Cove, NY
11542-2548
(516) 759-7000; Fax (516) 759-7014
Dealer guide and dealer referral service.

American Philatelic Society (APS)
P.O. Box 8000
State College, PA 16803
(814) 237-3803
Dealer guide.

DIRECTORIES

Where to Buy It Guide to the Stamp World
Krause Publications, Inc.
700 East State Street
Iola, WI 54990

Yellow Pages for Stamp Collectors
Linn's Stamp News
P.O. Box 29
Sidney, OH 45365

EXPERTIZING

American Philatelic Expertizing Service
P.O. Box 8000
State College, PA 16803
(814) 237-3803

Philatelic Foundation
501 Fifth Avenue,
Room 1901
New York, NY 10017
(212) 867-3699

MAGAZINES

American Philatelist
P.O. Box 8000
State College, PA 16803

Scott Stamp Monthly
P.O. Box 828
Sidney, OH 45365

U.S. Stamp News
P.O. Box 5050
White Plains, NY 10602

Stamps Auction News
85 Canisteo Street
Hornell, NY 14843
A digest of auction prices realized for U.S. stamps and selected foreign issues.

MUSEUMS

Cardinal Spellman Philatelic Museum
235 Wellsley Street
Weston, MA 02193
(617) 894-6735

Hall of Stamps
United States Postal Service
475 L'Enfant Plaza
Washington, DC 20260

National Postal Museum
Smithsonian Institution
2 Massachusetts Avenue, NE
Washington, DC 20560

NEWSPAPERS

Global Stamp News
(monthly)
P.O. Box 97
Sidney, OH 45365
Devoted to foreign stamps.

Linn's Stamp News (weekly)
P.O. Box 29
Sidney, OH 45365

Mekeel's Stamp News and Market Report (weekly)
P.O. Box 5050
White Plains, NY 10602

Stamp Collector (weekly)
700 East State Street
Iola, WI 54990

Stamps Magazine (weekly)
85 Canisteo Street
Hornell, NY 14843

Stamp Wholesaler
(bimonthly)
700 East State Street
Iola, WI 54990
Primarily for dealers, but anyone can subscribe.

PHILATELIC AGENCIES

Hundreds of foreign philatelic agencies exist, from which new issues can be purchased at face value; a sampling appears below. Complete listings are published from time to time in philatelic periodicals.

AUSTRALIA

Australian Philatelic Bureau
GPO Box 9988
Melbourne, Victoria 3001
Australia

GERMANY

Deutsche Post AG
Versandstelle für Postwertzeichen
Niederlassung Weiden
92632 Weiden
Germany

GREAT BRITAIN

British Philatelic Bureau
20 Brandon Street
Edinburgh EH3 5TT
Scotland

ITALY

Ufficio Principale Filatelico
Via Mario de Fiori 103/A
00187 Rome
Italy

JAPAN

Tokyo Central Post Office
Philatelic Section
CPO Box 888
Tokyo 100-91
Japan

U.S.A

Philatelic Fulfillment Service Center
United States Postal Service
Box 419636
Kansas City, MO
64179-0996
(800) 782-6724

PHILATELIC LIBRARIES

American Philatelic Research Library (APRL)
100 Oakwood Avenue
State College, PA 16803
(814) 237-3803; Fax (814) 237-6128

The Collectors Club
22 E. 35th Street
New York, NY 10016
(212) 683-0559

The Postal History Foundation
920 N. First Avenue
Tucson, AZ 85719
(602) 623-6652

Rocky Mountain Philatelic Library
CS 27 Box 906
8007 W. Colfax Avenue
Lakewood, CO 80215

San Diego County Philatelic Library
4133 Poplar Street
San Diego, CA 92105

Western Philatelic Library
655 W. Olive Avenue
Sunnyvale, CA 94086

Wineburgh Philatelic Research Library
University of Texas at Dallas
P.O. Box 830643
Richardson, TX 75083

PHILATELIC LITERATURE DEALERS

Philip T. Bansner, Inc.
P.O. Box 2529
West Lawn, PA 19609

PHILATELIC SOCIETIES

American First Day Cover Society (AFDCS)
P.O. Box 65960
Tuscon, AZ 85728-5960

American Philatelic Society (APS)
P.O. Box 8000
State College, PA 16803
(814) 237-3803

American Topical Association (ATA)
P.O. Box 630
Johnstown, PA 15907

Bureau Issues Association (BIA)
P.O. Box 23707
Belleville, IL 62223-0707

Errors, Freaks, Oddities Collectors Club (EFOCC)
138 Lakemont Drive East
Kingsland, GA 31548-8921
(800) 236-2128;
Fax (912) 729-1585

**Precancel Stamp Society
(PSS)**
P.O. Box 4072
Missoula, MT 59806

STAMP ALBUMS, MOUNTS, AND SUPPLIES

H. E. Harris & Co.
P.O. Box 817
Florence, AL 35631
Albums, mounts, supplies.

**Lighthouse Publications,
Inc.**
P.O. Box 705
Hackensack, NJ 07602
Albums, mounts, supplies.

Lindner Publications, Inc.
P.O. Box 5056
Syracuse, NY 13220
Albums, mounts, supplies.

Minkus Publications
10725 John Price Road
Charlotte, NC 28273
Albums and supplements.

Safe Publications, Inc.
P.O. Box 263
Southampton, PA 18966
Albums, mounts, supplies.

**Scott Publishing
Company**
P.O. Box 828
Sidney, OH 45365
Albums, mounts, supplies.

Washington Press
2 Vreeland Road
Florham Park, NJ 07932
*ArtCraft first day covers;
White Ace album pages;
Stampmounts.*

STAMP DEALERS (LOCAL)

Far too numerous to list. Consult your telephone Yellow Pages.

STAMP INSURANCE

**American Philatelic
Society Insurance Advisor**
P.O. Box 8000
State College, PA 16803

APPENDIX

GLOSSARY

aerogramme: a lightweight type of postal stationery with gummed flaps that can be folded and sealed for mailing. Aerogrammes are intended primarily for international airmail correspondence. Also called air letters.

airmail: a stamp intended primarily for use on airmail.

album: a book in which a collection of stamps or covers is mounted.

approvals: selections of stamps sent by mail, usually inexpensive singles or sets for the beginning or general collector. The collector purchases what he likes and returns the balance.

APO: army post office. *See* **FPO**.

APS: American Philatelic Society.

arrow block: a block of stamps on whose selvage appears an arrow-like marking that serves as a guide to assist printers in cutting press sheets apart at the time of production.

ASDA: American Stamp Dealers Association.

ATA: American Topical Association.

backstamp: a postmark placed on the reverse of a cover to indicate its arrival date or time.

bank mixture: mixture of stamps on paper, so called because it traditionally originated from bank correspondence. Bank mixtures are regarded as premium mixtures because they contain a large number of high-denomination and seldom encountered stamps.

BIA: Bureau Issues Association.

bisect: a stamp cut in half (often diagonally) and used as one-half the face value of the uncut stamp.

blind perforations: lightly impressed perforations that often give stamps the appearance of being imperforate. Stamps with blind perfs are not considered errors. Also called blind perfs.

block: four or more stamps arranged in a rectangle.

B-O-B: back of the book, includes stamps such as postage dues, special deliveries, and parcel posts-anything listed in the rear of the catalogue following definitives and commemoratives.

booklet pane: a small sheetlet of stamps bound between card-stock covers by staples, thread, or glue.

bourse: a show in which dealers take booths and offer their wares to the stamp-collecting public. Bourses are often held in conjunction with stamp shows or exhibitions.

bullseye cancel: a cancellation, usually circular, struck squarely on the center of the stamp, also known as socked on the nose.

bureau precancel: a precancel whose city and state overprint was applied at the Bureau of Engraving and Printing. *See* **local precancel**.

cachet: a decorative illustration printed on a cover, usually in connection with the first day of issue of a new stamp or some other special event. Cachets may be printed, rubber-stamped, hand-painted, or applied by any other means.

cancel: an obliterating mark applied to a stamp, thereby rendering it invalid for future use. Cancellations may be applied by handstamps, machine, or pen. *See* **postmark**.

canceled to order (CTO): cancellations applied by governments, often to full sheets. CTOs are sold in bulk to packet makers, approval dealers, etc.

catalogue: a reference work that lists, illustrates, and prices postage stamps. Stamp catalogues can be general or highly specialized.

CDS: circular date stamp. A circular postmark showing place of mailing together with date and, in some cases, time.

centering: the position of a stamp's design in relation to its perforations or the edges of a stamp. Well-centered stamps possess even margins all around.

cinderella: a general, all-encompassing term applied to any stamplike item not valid for postage, such as exhibition labels, and Christmas seals. Anything that looks like a postage stamp but is not.

classic: an early issue, usually nineteenth-century.

coil stamps: stamps issued in rolls. Coil stamps contain straightedges on two sides.

commemorative: a special stamp issued in honor of a specific event, personality or anniversary, typically available for a limited time only.

commercial cover: a cover used for business correspondence (although more recently any cover of a nonphilatelic nature) without any philatelic intent, as opposed to one created for some philatelic purpose. *See* **philatelic cover.**

computer-vended postage: stamps dispensed by vending machines that imprint the denomination at the time the stamp is vended, usually on security paper containing a preprinted background.

corner card: the return address on the upper left corner of a cover.

cover: philatelic term for an envelope, almost always implying that it has gone through the mail.

cut square: a piece containing the postage imprint cut from postal stationery, usually to facilitate mounting in an album. *See* **entire.**

dead country: a country that no longer issues postage stamps, most often because of changing political reality, such as with former colonies (Belgian Congo, Mozambique Company) or absorption (East Germany, Confederate States of America).

definitive: a stamp, usually part of a series, available over an extended period of time for use on everyday mail. Definitives are also known as regular issues.

dry gum: non-glossy gum that is flat in appearance, as opposed to "wet" gum, which is glossy or shiny in appearance. Also referred to as matte gum or dull gum.

duck stamp: a waterfowl-hunting stamp.

EFO: errors, freaks, and oddities. A term applied to stamps with random minor production irregularities such as misaligned perforations, freak perforations, printing offset on reverse, and ink smears.

EKU: earliest known use. The earliest date a stamp is known to have been used.

entire: a complete item of postal stationery.

error: usually refers to a stamp with a major production error, e.g., a stamp lacking perforations, a stamp with a design element inverted, or a stamp with a color or colors omitted. Minor production irregularities are referred to as EFOs. Stamps with design errors (such as the wrong number of stars on a flag) are generally not considered "errors."

essay: an unadopted stamp design, either an entire design not used, or a design very similar to the issued design except for small modifications.

expert certificate: a certificate issued by an acknowledged expert or expertizing body attesting to the genuineness or non-genuineness of a stamp or cover.

expert mark: a mark of authentication placed on the reverse of a stamp or on a cover by a recognized expert.

exploded: refers to a booklet that has been dissembled into individual panes.

face value: a stamp's denomination.

fake: an outright forgery; also a stamp (or cover) that has been modified to improve its value or desirability with the intent of defrauding a buyer.

fancy cancel: a cancellation featuring a pictorial device or geometric design, often carved from cork by nineteenth-century postmasters, but also used well into the twentieth century.

fault: any defect affecting the appearance or integrity of a stamp such as a tear, cut, crease, thin, scrape, stain, scuff, fold, pinhole, or foxing.

favor cancel: a cancellation applied to a stamp or cover as a favor by a postal employee, often on an item that might not normally have been used on mail or have gone through the mail, or with a postmarking device not normally used for that issue.

first day cover (FDC): a cover, usually cacheted, postmarked on the first day a stamp is available for sale.

first flight cover: a cover, usually cacheted, carried on the first flight of a new airmail route.

foxing: rust-colored discoloration caused by microorganisms.

FPO: fleet post office.

grill: a waffle-like pattern impressed into some nineteenth-century stamps to break their paper fibers and make them more receptive to postmarking ink. Used to prevent the removal of cancellations and reuse of stamps.

gutter: the space between two panes of stamps on a sheet.

heavily hinged (HH): hinged with strong glue that has disturbed gum or will disturb it when removed.

hinge: a stamp hinge. A small piece of paper or glassine used to attach a stamp to an album page.

imperforate: lacking perforations.

inscription block: a block of stamps on whose selvage appears a printed inscription.

intaglio: a method of printing in which the design is engraved (recessed) into a metal plate. Ink fills the recesses and, when the stamp is printed, forms small ridges, which can be detected by magnifying glass or by running a finger over the design and feeling the ridges.

international reply coupon (IRC): a coupon good for one single-rate surface letter stamp. Coupons may be purchased or redeemed in any UPU member nation. Used to enable an individual in one country to send postage for a reply to an individual in another country.

invert: a stamp with an element of the design upside down in relation to the other elements of the design.

job lot: a mishmash consisting of just about anything—loose stamps, covers, album pages, mixtures, mint sets, remainders, etc.—often sold by the carton. Dealers often dispose of surplus, disorganized material in the form of job lots. Sometimes called a mystery lot.

joint issue: stamps of two (or more) countries featuring a similar design, issued in collaboration with one another specifically to commemorate something important to both.

kiloware: mixture of stamps on paper sold by the pound or kilogram, hence the name.

lightly hinged (LH): hinged so that the hinge mark is barely noticeable.

line pair: a pair of coil stamps on which a line appears between the stamps. On engraved, rotary-press coil stamps, lines are created by ink that fills the space where the curved plates join and is then printed in the same fashion as ink from recesses in an intaglio stamp design.

local precancel: a precancel whose city and state overprint was applied locally rather than at the Bureau of Engraving and Printing. *See* **bureau precancel.**

local stamp: a stamp issued by a private firm to evidence payment of fee for conveyance of mail to the nearest post office.

manuscript cancel: handwritten cancellation.

maximum card: a postcard bearing the same illustration or design as the stamp affixed to it and cancelled with first-day or commemorative cancellation.

meter: a stamp printed by a postage meter machine such as those made by the Pitney-Bowes company.

mint: an unused stamp with full original gum as issued by the post office.

mission mixture: a mixture of stamps on paper so called because their traditional source was religious or charitable organizations.

mounts: clear plastic pouches or containers used to protect stamps and affix them to album pages.

multiple: a group of two or more unseparated stamps, such as a block, pair, strip, or pane.

never hinged (NH): a stamp that has never been hinged.

new issue: newly issued stamps, often received by subscription either directly from a postal administration or from a stamp dealer.

off-center: a stamp on which the design is poorly centered in relation to the perforations.

official stamp: a stamp valid for use only by a government agency and intended for use only on official mail.

off paper: used stamps that have been soaked off paper. Most often applied to mixtures, which are sold either "on paper" or "off paper."

on cover: a stamp attached to a cover.

on paper: *See* **off paper.**

on piece: a stamp attached to a piece of paper torn or cut from an envelope or wrapper.

original gum (OG): gum applied to a stamp at the time of manufacture.

overprint: printing applied to stamps after regular production, typically to denote a special purpose (such as airmail), to commemorate something, as a control measure, etc. *See* **surcharge.**

packet: typically a printed window envelope containing an assortment of stamps for the beginner or general collector.

packet material: common, inexpensive stamps.

pair: two unseparated stamps.

pane: a finished "sheet" of stamps as purchased across a post office counter, as distinct from a press or production sheet, which usually contains multiple panes of stamps.

perfin: short for perforated initials. Refers to a stamp with initials or a design punched in it by perforating device. Perfins are utilized by firms (most frequently) and governments (occasionally) to identify stamps in order to prevent pilferage or unauthorized use.

perforations: the series of holes punched between stamps to facilitate their separation. The size of the holes and spacing vary from issue to issue. Perforations are measured by a perforation gauge.

permit imprint: printed indicia used by permit-holding bulk mailers to evidence payment of postage.

philatelic cover: a cover prepared and sent by or for a stamp collector, often with stamps or combinations of stamps not normally encountered on mail, such as complete sets of semi-postals. *See* commercial cover.

plate block: a block of stamps with the printing plate number(s) appearing on the selvage. The size of a plate block can vary from issue to issue.

plate number coil (PNC): A coil stamp on which a small printing plate number appears at the bottom. Plate numbers appear at the bottom of every nth stamp, typically every 24 or 52 stamps.

postal card: a card with postage imprinted on it by the postal service.

postal stationery: stationery sold by a postal service usually, but not always, with imprinted postage. Postal stationery includes postal cards, stamped envelopes, and aerogrammes.

postcard: a privately produced card without postage imprinted on it and usually containing a printed greeting or view on the reverse.

postmark: an official marking (usually circular but can be any shape or in manuscript or, most recently, sprayed-on dot-matrix style characters) applied to a piece of mail, most often indicating date and place of mailing. Postmarks are often used to cancel stamps.

postmaster's provisional: a stamp issued by a postmaster. Generally refers to those issued during the period between the enactment of uniform postage by Congress in 1845 and the first U.S. postage stamps in 1847.

precancel: a stamp canceled prior to use either by printed or by hand-applied marking, most typically with the name of a city and state between two parallel bars, but later with only parallel bars or with the class of service between parallel bars. For use by permit-holding bulk mailers. *See* **service-inscribed.**

private treaty: an arrangement in which a stamp dealer acts in the capacity of agent for a seller, receiving a commission for his services.

proof: a trial impression made from a die or plate before regular production in order to check engraving, color, etc.

regummed: a stamp that has had new gum applied to simulate its original gum.

reissue: a stamp that has been printed from original plates and released subsequent to becoming obsolete. *See* **reprint.**

reperforated: a stamp that has had perforations added to a straightedge or to a perforated edge that has been trimmed to improve centering.

reprint: a stamp that has been printed from new plates (often distinguishable from the original plates) and released subsequent to becoming obsolete. *See* **reissue.**

roulette: a philatelic term referring to a series of small slits applied between stamps to facilitate separation.

secret mark: a small, difficult-to-detect engraver's mark applied to designs so that stamps printed by one source (such as the Continental Bank Note Company) could be distinguished from identical stamps printed by another source (such as the National Bank Note Company).

selvage: the marginal area surrounding a sheet or pane of stamps. Sometimes spelled "selvedge."

semipostal: a postage stamp for which only part of the purchase price applies toward postage; the balance is collected for some other purpose, often a charitable cause. Semipostals are usually denominated by two figures, the first applying toward postage, the second toward the other purpose, e.g., 50c+20c.

series: a group of stamps, usually definitives, sharing a theme or motif, and often issued over a period of time ranging from months to years, and usually in use for a number of years.

service-inscribed: a type of stamp used by bulk mailers on which the class of service is inscribed (printed) at time of production. Referred to as precancels by some, however the printed inscription usually appears to be the part of the design rather than a cancellation.

set: two or more stamps sharing a similar theme, motif, or appearance, usually commemoratives, usually issued at the same time, and usually, but not always, of different denominations.

se-tenant: two or more different stamp designs printed next to one another on a pane of stamps, a souvenir sheet, a booklet, or a coil.

short set: an incomplete set of stamps, usually comprised of only the lower denominations.

socked on the nose: *see* **bullseye cancel.**

sound: free of faults.

souvenir card: a card containing printed examples of stamps (or currency). Souvenir cards are usually issued in connection with a stamp show or stamp event. Souvenir cards are produced by both the government and private entities. Stamps appearing on souvenir cards are not valid for postage.

souvenir sheet: a sheet, usually small, containing one or more stamps, usually bearing a commemorative marginal inscription, and usually issued for a special event or occasion.

space filler: a damaged or otherwise normally uncollectible copy of a stamp good for no other purpose than filling an album space until a collectible copy comes along. Often used to imply that a stamp has little or no value.

stampless cover: a cover sent through the mail without postage stamps, the payment of postage evidenced by handstamp or manuscript. Usually refers to covers before the advent of postage stamps.

strip: three or more unseparated stamps arranged side-to-side or end-to-end.

supplement: an installment of album pages to bring a loose-leaf album up to date, usually published annually.

surcharge: an overprint that changes the face value of a stamp or piece of postal stationery. *See* **overprint.**

tab: a piece of selvage attached to an individual stamp.

tagging: a luminescent coating applied to stamps during printing. Usually invisible to the naked eye, tagging can be observed under ultraviolet light. Tagging may cover all or part of a stamp.

tête-bêche: two adjacent stamps, one of which is inverted in relation to the other. From the French, meaning "head-to-foot."

tied: indicates that a single cancellation strike falls on both stamp and cover. Such a stamp is said to be "tied to cover."

transit mark: a marking applied to a cover at a point along its journey.

Universal Postal Union (UPU): international postal governing body to which all recognized nations belong, which administers postal treaties and the transmission of mail between member states. Founded in 1863.

unlisted: not recognized by a catalogue publisher as being a postage stamp, by virtue of either having been issued by an entity not recognized as a legitimate government or not having been issued for postal purposes.

view card: a commercially produced card containing a view (landscapes, motels, or often humor, messages, or greetings) and usually sold or given as a souvenir. Also called a picture postcard.

wallpaper: common, inexpensive, colorful stamps of the type sold in bulk and having little individual value.

watermark: a design impressed into paper during its manufacture, sometimes visible when held up to light, but most often visible when immersed in watermark fluid.

wet gum: gum that is shiny or glossy in appearance, as opposed to "dry" gum, which is flat in appearance.

BIBLIOGRAPHY

CATALOGUES

Brookman United States, United Nations & Canada Stamps & Postal Collectibles. Krause Publications, 700 East State Street, Iola, WI 54990. *Catalogue price list, published annually.*

Durland Standard Plate Number Catalog. Bureau Issues Association, P.O. Box 23707, Belleville, IL 62223.

Harris US/BNA Postage Stamp Catalog. H. E. Harris & Co., P.O. Box 817, Florence, AL 35631. *Catalogue/price list for U.S. and British North America, published annually.*

Minkus Specialized American Stamp Catalog. Novus Debut Inc., 10725 John Price Road, Charlotte, NC 28273. *Catalogue of U.S. stamps.*

Mystic U.S. Stamp Catalogue. Mystic Stamp Company, 24 Mill Street, Camden, NY 13116-9111. *Catalogue of U.S. stamps featuring full-color illustrations.*

Planty Photo Encyclopedia of Cacheted First Day Covers. Earl Planty. Michael A. Mellone, P.O. Box 206, Stewartsville, NJ 08886. *Highly detailed multi-volume catalogue on cacheted FDCs of the classic period, 1901–1939.*

The Postal Service Guide to U.S. Stamps. United States Postal Service, Box 419636, Kansas City, MO 64179-0996. *Also available over the counter at many post offices.*

Sanabria Airmail Catalogue. Sanabria, Inc., P.O. Box 402, Loveland, CO 80539. *Catalogue of airmail stamps of the world.*

Scott Specialized Catalogue of U.S. Stamps. Scott Publishing Co., P.O. Box 828, Sidney, OH 45365. *Published annually.*

Scott Standard Postage Stamp Catalogue. Scott Publishing Co., P.O. Box 828, Sidney, OH 45365. *Multi-volume set covering stamps of the world, published annually.*

Scott U.S. First Day Cover Catalogue and Checklist. Mike Mellone. Scott Publishing Co., P.O. Box 828, Sidney, OH 45365. *Published annually.*

Town & Type Catalogue, 5th Edition. Precancel Stamp Society, PSS Catalogs, 108 Ashswamp Road, Scarborough, ME 04074. *Complete listing of all recognized U.S. precancels.*

U.S. Errors: Inverts, Imperforates, and Colors Omitted on United States Postage Stamps. Sanabria, Inc., P.O. Box 402, Loveland, CO 80539. *Catalogue of major errors on U.S. stamps. Published biennially.*

ELECTRONIC MEDIA

The Encyclopedia of U.S. Postage Stamps. Richard L. Sine. ZCI Publishing Co., 1950 Stemmons, Suite 4044, Dallas, TX 75207. *CD-ROM of U.S. stamps.*

GENERAL READING

Basic Philately. Kenneth A. Wood. Krause Publications, Inc., 700 East State Street, Iola, WI 54990.

Franklin D. Roosevelt & the Stamps of the United States 1933-45. Brian C. Baur. Linn's Stamp News, P.O. Box 29, Sidney, OH 45365.

Fundamentals of Philately. L. N. Williams. American Philatelic Society, P.O. Box 8000, State College, PA 16803.

The Inverted Jenny: Mystery, Money Mania. George Amick. Amos Press, Inc., P.O. Box 29, Sidney, OH 45365. *The most thorough account of the famous inverted Jenny.*

Linn's U.S. Stamp Yearbook. Linn's Stamp News, P.O. Box 29, Sidney, OH 45365. *Published annually, gives details regarding design, production, problems, etc., for each stamp issued that year.*

More of the World's Greatest Stamp Collectors. Stanley M. Bierman. Linn's Stamp News, P.O. Box 29, Sidney, OH 45365.

Nassau Street. Herman Herst, Jr. Amos Press, Inc., P.O. Box 29, Sidney, OH 45365. *Enjoyable memoir of a stamp dealer active during the golden era of philately. One of philately's best-selling books.*

On the Road: The Quest for Stamps. Stephen R. Datz. General Philatelic Corporation, P.O. Box 402, Loveland, CO 80539. *Insights into the stamp business by a dealer who has traveled America buying collections.*

Philatelic Forgers: Their Lives and Works. Varro E. Tyler. Linn's Stamp News, P.O. Box 29, Sidney, OH 45365.

Still More Stories to Collect Stamps By. Herman Herst, Jr. Mekeel's Stamp News, P.O. Box 5050, White Plains, NY 10602. *More stories by the author of* Nassau Street.

The Wild Side: Philatelic Mischief, Murder, and Intrigue. Stephen R. Datz. General Philatelic Corporation, P.O. Box 402, Loveland, CO 80539. *A stamp dealer's firsthand experiences with philatelic rogues and scoundrels.*

The World's Greatest Stamp Collectors. Stanley M. Bierman. Linn's Stamp News, P.O. Box 29, Sidney, OH 45365. *Highly readable biographies of the world's greatest stamp collectors.*

REFERENCE GUIDES

American Stamp Dealers Association Membership Guide. American Stamp Dealers Association, 3 School Street, Glen Cove, NY 11452-2548. *Cross-referenced by specialty.*

The Buyer's Guide: An Analysis of Selected U.S. Postage Stamps. Stephen R. Datz. General Philatelic Corporation, P.O. Box 402, Loveland, CO 80539. *Highly detailed stamp-by-stamp analysis of better U.S. stamps, including premium characteristics, gum and hinging, fakes and problem stamps, when to expertize, etc. Completely illustrated.*

The Expert's Book. Paul W. Schmid. Palm Press, P.O. Box 373, Huntington, NY 11743. *Superb in-depth analysis of the U.S. Washington-Franklin series, including all fakes and forgeries. Completely illustrated.*

How to Detect Damaged, Altered, and Repaired Stamps. Paul W. Schmid. Krause Publications, Inc., 700 East State Street, Iola, WI 54990. *The most authoritative and easy-to-use book on the subject of altered U.S. stamps. Well illustrated.*

Linn's Plate Number Coil Handbook. Ken Lawrence. Linn's Stamp News, P.O. Box 29, Sidney, OH 45365.

Mekeel's U.S. Reference Manual. Mekeel's Stamp News, P.O. Box 5050, White Plains, NY 10602. *In-depth look at selected U.S. special-interest stamps and covers, including rarities and difficult-to-identify items.*

Micarelli Identification Guide to U.S. Stamps. Charles Micarelli. Scott Publishing Co., P.O. Box 828, Sidney, OH 45365. *Comprehensive identification guide to U.S. definitive stamps, fully illustrated, and especially useful for hard-to-identify nineteenth-century issues.*

Post Dates. Kenneth A. Wood. Krause Publications, Inc., 700 East State Street, Iola, WI 54990. *A chronology of intriguing events in the mails and philately beginning with the year 4,000 B.C.*

StampFinder Stamp Selection Guides. USID, Inc., 6175 N.W. 153rd St., Suite 221, Miami Lakes, FL 33014. *Investment-oriented stamp price performance guides. Volumes include U.S. and Canada; British Commonwealth; Mexico and South America; Germany and German Colonies; and the Far East.*

This Is Philately: An Encyclopedia of Stamp Collecting. Kenneth A. Wood. Krause Publications, Inc., 700 East State Street, Iola, WI 54990. *Superb three-volume reference covering every conceivable aspect of philately.*

Top Dollar Paid: The Complete Guide to Selling Your Stamps. Stephen R. Datz. General Philatelic Corporation, P.O. Box 402, Loveland, CO 80539. *This how-to guide includes selling in person, by phone or mail, negotiating, getting the best price, tactics to avoid, specifics on valuation, and more.*

Where in the World? Krause Publications, Inc., 700 East State Street, Iola, WI 54990. *Atlas of stamp issuing-entities since 1840.*